Scott, Foresman Reading

Hidden Wonders

Program Authors

Ira E. Aaron
Dauris Jackson
Carole Riggs
Richard G. Smith
Robert J. Tierney

Book Authors

Ira E. Aaron
Rena Koke

Instructional Consultants

John Manning
Dolores Perez

Scott, Foresman and Company
Editoral Offices: Glenview, Illinois

Regional Offices: Palo Alto, California
Tucker, Georgia • Glenview, Illinois
Oakland, New Jersey • Dallas, Texas

ACKNOWLEDGMENTS

YOU LOOK RIDICULOUS by Bernard Waber, published by Houghton Mifflin Company. Copyright © 1966 by Bernard Waber. Reprinted by permission of the publisher.

"What Am I?" from HELLO AND GOOD–BY by Mary Ann Hoberman. Copyright © 1959 by Mary Ann Hoberman. Reprinted by permission of Russell & Volkening, Inc. as agents for the author.

"Sally Ride: Scientist-Astronaut" from "Sally Ride: Scientist-Astronaut" by Molly Tyson. Copyright © 1978, HIGHLIGHTS FOR CHILDREN, INC. Columbus, Ohio. Reprinted by permission of the publisher.

"Pecos Bill Rides a Tornado" from "Pecos Bill Rides a Tornado" by Wyatt Blassingame. Copyright 1973 by Wyatt Blassingame. Reprinted with the permission of Garrard Publishing Co., Champaign, Illinois.

"Birthday" and "Sing for Joy" adapted from DELILAH by Carole Hart. Text copyright © 1973 by Carole Hart. By permission of Harper & Row, Publishers, Inc. and McIntosh and Otis, Inc.

"Tuesday I Was Ten" from DON'T EVER CROSS A CROCODILE by Kaye Starbird. Copyright © 1963 by Kaye Starbird. Reprinted by permission of Paul R. Reynolds, Inc., 12 East 41st Street, New York 10017.

"How Is a Table Like You?" consists of excerpts from NAILHEADS & POTATO EYES by Cynthia Basil. Copyright © 1976 by Cynthia Basil. By permission of William Morrow & Company.

"Somebody Stole Second" adapted from SOMEBODY STOLE SECOND by Louise Munro Foley. Copyright © 1972 by Louise Munro Foley. Reprinted by permission of Delacorte Press.

Photographs in "The Dance Theatre of Harlem" are used by permission of The Dance Theatre of Harlem and the following people: Martha Swope, New York City (for

ISBN 0-673-21411-7

photograph of Arthur Mitchell teaching the junior company); © Jack Vartoogian, NYC. All Rights Reserved. (for photographs of two dancers and Arthur Mitchell in rehearsal with the company); all other photographs are by Marbeth.

"Tall Tina" from TALL TINA by Muriel Stanek. Copyright by Muriel Stanek. Reprinted by permission of the author.

"Pooh Goes Visiting" from WINNIE–THE–POOH by A. A. Milne, illustrated by Ernest H. Shepard. Copyright 1926 by E. P. Dutton & Co., Inc., renewal © 1954 by A. A. Milne. Reprinted by permission of the publishers, E. P. Dutton, The Canadian Publishers, McClelland and Stewart Limited, Toronto, Methuen Children's Books Ltd., and Curtis Brown Ltd.

MARY OF MILE 18. © 1971 Ann Blades, published in the U.S. and Canada by Tundra Books and in the U.K. and elsewhere in the British Commonwealth by The Bodley Head. Reprinted by permission of the publishers.

"My Puppy" from UP THE WINDY HILL by Aileen Fisher. Reprinted by permission of Scott, Foresman and Company.

"The Three Wonderful Seeds" by Gloria Logan. Reprinted from HUMPTY DUMPTY'S MAGAZINE. Copyright © 1961 by Parents' Magazine Enterprises, a division of Gruner + Jahr, U.S.A., Inc.

"Peter's Brownstone House" is an abridgment and adaptation of PETER'S BROWNSTONE HOUSE by Hila Colman. Copyright © 1963 by Hila Colman. By permission of William Morrow & Company and Hila Colman.

"Chameleon Was a Spy" consists of the adapted text and selected illustrations from CHAMELEON WAS A SPY, written and illustrated by Diane Redfield Massie. Copyright © 1979 by Diane Redfield Massie. By permission of Thomas Y. Crowell, Publishers and Diane Redfield Massie.

Excerpted by permission of G. P. Putnam's Sons from "Hiding" from EVERYTHING & ANYTHING by Dorothy Aldis. Copyright 1925, 1926, 1927; Renewed © 1953, 1954, 1955 by Dorothy Aldis.

Adapted by permission of G. P. Putnam's Sons and William Morris Agency from THE ULTIMATE AUTO by Patrick McGivern. Copyright © 1969 by Patrick McGivern.

Reprinted with permission from the book THE BICYCLE AND HOW IT WORKS by David Urquhart, copyright 1972 by David Urquhart. Published by David McKay Co., Inc.

Text and illustrations developed and produced by Curriculum Concepts under the direction of Scott, Foresman and Company.

(Acknowledgments continued on page 352)

CONTENTS

4

SECTION ONE

You Look Ridiculous

by Bernard Waber

Once upon a time in the jungle, a rhinoceros came upon a hippopotamus splashing about in the mud.

"You look ridiculous," said the rhinoceros to the hippopotamus.

"But I like mud," answered the hippopotamus.

"Oh, it isn't the mud that makes you look ridiculous," said the rhinoceros. "It's your nose."

The hippopotamus looked down at her nose. "What's wrong with my nose?" she asked.

"You don't see anything missing?" the rhinoceros asked.

The hippopotamus shook her head.

8

"You don't see a horn missing?" the rhinoceros asked again.

"A horn?" said the hippopotamus.

"A horn," said the rhinoceros. "Your nose doesn't have a horn and a nose without a horn looks absolutely ridiculous."

Raising herself from the mud, the hippopotamus looked down at her nose once more. When she looked up again, the rhinoceros was gone.

"If only I had a horn, like the rhinoceros, I wouldn't look ridiculous," thought the hippopotamus. That's the way it was with the hippopotamus. Once a worrisome thought was put into her head, she would fret and fuss and fume and just never let go of it.

There was only one way to settle it, she decided. She would go and ask everyone she met if they too thought she looked ridiculous. First she met a lion. "Do you think I look ridiculous?" she asked the lion.

The lion thought about it. "Well, if it's an honest opinion you want . . ." the lion began at last.

"Yes," said the hippopotamus.

"Then I must say you do look ridiculous. Look at you," said the lion. "You haven't got a mane. What you need is a glorious mane like mine." The lion shook his mane just to prove how truly glorious it was. "No hard feelings, I hope," said the lion.

"No hard feelings," answered the hippopotamus sadly.

"If only I had a glorious mane, like the lion, I wouldn't look ridiculous," thought the hippopotamus, continuing her walk.

She met a leopard. "Do you think I look ridiculous?" she asked the leopard.

The leopard studied the hippopotamus carefully. "Now that you mention it . . ." the leopard began.

"Yes," said the hippopotamus.

"I would say you do look ridiculous. Look at you," said the leopard. "You have no spots. What you need is a handsomely spotted coat like mine."

The leopard gave a good, long stretch to show off every last spot on his handsome coat. "We're still friends, I hope," said the leopard.

"We're still friends," answered the hippopotamus sadly.

"If only I had handsome spots, like the leopard, I wouldn't look ridiculous," thought the hippopotamus, continuing her walk.

She met an elephant. "Do you think I look ridiculous?" she asked the elephant.

The elephant seemed surprised by the question. "I have to think about it," he said.

The hippopotamus waited while the elephant thought.

"Aha," said the elephant, "I know what it is."

"What?" asked the hippopotamus eagerly.

"You have no ears."

"No ears?" said the hippopotamus.

"No ears to speak of," said the elephant. "What you need are big, floppy ears like mine."

The elephant flopped his ears to prove his point. "See what I mean?" said the elephant.

"I see," answered the hippopotamus sadly. "If only I had big, floppy ears, like the elephant, I wouldn't look ridiculous," thought the hippopotamus, continuing her walk.

12

She met a monkey. "Do you think I look ridiculous?" she asked the monkey.

"If you call not having a tail ridiculous, then I would say you look ridiculous," answered the monkey.

"No tail?" said the hippopotamus.

"No tail to speak of," said the monkey. "Look at me," continued the monkey. "I am not nearly your size and I have a magnificent tail."

With that, the monkey scrambled up on a tree and swung from a branch by his tail. "Nothing personal, of course," the monkey called down.

"Of course not," the hippopotamus answered sadly.

14

"If only I had a magnificent tail, like the monkey, I wouldn't look ridiculous," thought the hippopotamus, continuing her walk.

She met a giraffe. "Do you think I look ridiculous?" she asked the giraffe.

"Of course you look ridiculous," said the giraffe, getting to the point at once. "You have no neck."

"No neck?" said the hippopotamus.

"No neck to speak of," said the giraffe. "How can you possibly see the world without a neck?"

"I see flowers, I see birds, I see the stars at night . . ." began the hippopotamus.

"Ah, but do you see the treetops? Do you see the distant hills? Of course not," said the giraffe, answering her own questions. "What you need is a long, long neck like mine."

With that the giraffe stretched out her neck until it seemed her head would disappear into the clouds and she went about the business of seeing the world. "I think you're very nice otherwise," the giraffe called back over her shoulder.

"Thank you," answered the hippopotamus sadly.

"If only I had a long, long neck, like the giraffe, I wouldn't look ridiculous," thought the hippopotamus, continuing her walk.

She met a turtle. "Do you think I look ridiculous?" she asked the turtle.

"I suppose someone should tell you," said the turtle.

"Yes," said the hippopotamus.

"You do look ridiculous without a shell."

"A shell?" said the hippopotamus.

"Oh, they're wonderful," said the turtle.
"I couldn't live without one. My shell is my
house. It keeps me warm when it is cold and
cool when it is hot. And if I ever need a place
to hide," said the turtle, backing into her
shell, "I know exactly where to go. You'd have
found out sooner or later," the turtle called
out from inside her little house.

"I suppose," answered the hippopotamus sadly.
"If only I had a wonderful shell, like the
turtle, I wouldn't look ridiculous," thought the
hippopotamus, continuing her walk.

She met a nightingale. "Do you think I look ridiculous?" she asked the nightingale.

"If you don't mind my saying so, I think you sound ridiculous," said the nightingale. "What you need is a beautiful voice like mine. Listen," said the nightingale. And the nightingale sang a beautiful but sad song for the hippopotamus.

Suddenly the hippopotamus could not bear to continue her walk or ask further questions. "I am a ridiculous creature," she sighed. "I shall find a place to hide and never show myself to anyone again."

The hippopotamus ran and ran until she found a lonely place where no one would find her. "Why did I have to be born looking so ridiculous?" she cried as she fell asleep that night. While sleeping she began to dream. And as so often happens in dreams, her dearest of wishes were granted.

She dreamed she had a horn like the rhinoceros's, a mane like the lion's, spots like the leopard's, ears like the elephant's, a tail like the monkey's, a neck like the giraffe's, a shell like the turtle's, and a voice like the nightingale's.

So delighted was the hippopotamus with her new appearance she ran to show herself off to everyone. "Look at me," she called out in her sweet nightingale voice, "I no longer look ridiculous."

18

Everyone laughed when they saw the new hippopotamus. The monkey laughed so hard he almost fell out of his tree.

"What is wrong?" cried the hippopotamus. "Why do you laugh? Can't you see for yourselves I no longer look ridiculous?"

This only made the animals laugh even more. The hippopotamus rushed to a rain puddle to see for herself. "Ohhh . . ." she cried out upon seeing herself, "I LOOK RIDICULOUS." She was so shaken by what she saw, she shook herself awake.

"Thank goodness it was only a dream," the hippopotamus sighed with relief. Joyfully she plopped herself into the nearest mudhole and from that day to this, is proud to be just what she is—a big, fat, wonderful hippopotamus.

Comprehension Check

1. What did the rhinoceros tell the hippopotamus that she was missing?
2. Why did the hippopotamus run to a lonely place where no one would find her?
3. Do you think the animals in the jungle were mean to the hippopotamus? Why or why not?
4. Pretend you overheard the conversation between the lion and the hippopotamus. What would you have said to the hippopotamus?

Literary Unit

What Am I?

by Mary Ann Hoberman

If I were as big as a lion,
If I were as small as a flea,
If I were as wide as a whiskery walrus,
What in the world would I be?

If I were as old as a tortoise,
If I were as young as a bee,
If I were as long as a silvery snake,
What in the world would I be?

If I were as smooth as a slippery eel,
If I were as smooth as a flippery seal,
If I were as strong as a lumbering ox
Or as shy as a deer
Or as sly as a fox
Or as wise as an owl
Or as dumb as a fowl
Or as smart as a dog
Or as plump as a hog
Or as lumpy-lump-lump as a bump on a log
Or if I were as nice as a nice milky cow
Or as stout all about as a pot-bellied sow
Well, I'd certainly be
A sight to see
But I wouldn't
     I wouldn't
        I wouldn't be me!

Fact or Fiction?

Do you know the difference between fact and fiction? Something is a fact if it is known to be true. Something is a **fact** if it can be proven to be true. Something is **fiction** if it is made up or imagined. Read the next paragraph.

Winter was on its way. Mervin the raccoon knew that for sure. When he woke up in the morning, his nose was very cold.
"Brrr," he said. He put on his earmuffs and woolly hat. "Summer is never long enough!" he exclaimed.

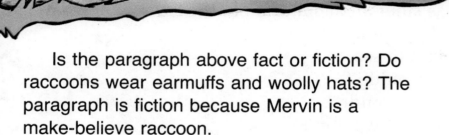

Is the paragraph above fact or fiction? Do raccoons wear earmuffs and woolly hats? The paragraph is fiction because Mervin is a make-believe raccoon.

Now read this paragraph.

In 1885 France gave the United States a wonderful gift. It is called the Statue of Liberty. You can climb up the narrow stairs inside the statue. You can see New York City from the top.

Is the second paragraph fact or fiction? The paragraph is fact because the information is true. You can check the information in another book, such as an encyclopedia.

Practice

1. Which paragraph below is probably fact? Why do you think so? What could you do to make sure?
2. Which paragraph is probably fiction? How do you know?

A. Barbara found a giant apple tree. The apples were purple. They looked good. Barbara reached out to pick one of the apples. "Hey!" cried the huge apple. "What are you doing?"

B. Stars in the sky are not all the same. Some stars are hotter than others. Some stars are white or blue. Other stars, such as the sun, are yellow. Still others are green or orange.

As you read the next story, "Sally Ride: Scientist-Astronaut," decide if it is fact or fiction.

Sally Ride:
Scientist-Astronaut

by Molly Tyson

When Sally Ride was ten years old, she had
no idea that she would someday grow up to be
one of America's first women astronauts. In
fact, if you had asked her then what she wanted
to be, she would have said, "I want to play
shortstop for the Los Angeles Dodgers." Sally
collected baseball cards by the boxful, and she
knew the name and batting average of every
player in the National League.

When Sally was twelve, her father and mother talked her into taking tennis lessons. At first she hated to trade in her baseball bat for a tennis racket, but it wasn't long before she started to win tournaments in her new sport. Soon a row of trophies replaced her box of baseball cards, and tennis star Billie Jean King replaced Dodger shortstop Maury Wills as her sports idol.

Sally first became interested in becoming an astronaut when astronaut John Glenn orbited the earth for the first time. Although Sally was only a young girl at the time, she remembers that day as if it were yesterday. So the girl who memorized batting averages and won tennis tournaments became a space fan too.

She quickly learned the name of every astronaut in the National Aeronautics and Space Administration (or NASA). She memorized the date of every launch and the name and number of every spacecraft from Freedom 7 to Skylab 3. Sally could tell you the speed of light, the distance to the moon, and the names of the three nearest stars (the sun, Alpha Centauri, and Barnard's star).

By the time she was sixteen, Sally had decided to become an astrophysicist, a scientist who studies space. She had also become a well-known tennis player. She remembers yawning through an important tennis match after staying up all night to watch Neil Armstrong's first steps on the moon. Sally lost that match.

As Sally got older many of her friends
started playing professional tennis. Some of
them tried to talk her into quitting school to
join them in playing professional tennis. But
Sally said no. Now she knows that she made
the right choice.

Sally helped pay her way through college by
teaching tennis at a summer camp owned by
Billie Jean King. After eight years of studies,
Sally became Dr. Sally Ride, the proud holder of
a Ph.D. degree in astrophysics from Stanford
University. Her plan was to become a college
professor.

NASA hired scientist-astronauts in 1965 to conduct experiments in space. Until that time all of the astronauts had been jet pilots. In 1976 NASA decided to hire more scientist-astronauts to conduct the experiments. They invited men and women from all over the country to apply for the job. Many scientists wrote letters saying that they wanted to be astronauts. One of them was Sally Ride.

Sally wasn't worried about passing NASA's physical fitness test. She was still in good shape from playing tennis, and she had been running eight miles a day. She knew that she was a good scientist, but so were many of the other people who had applied. How many would be picked? Who would they be?

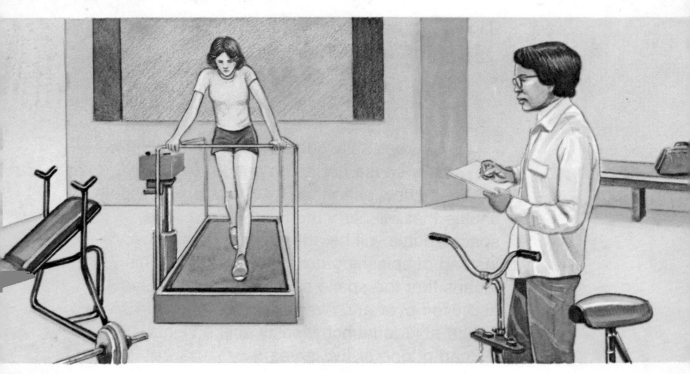

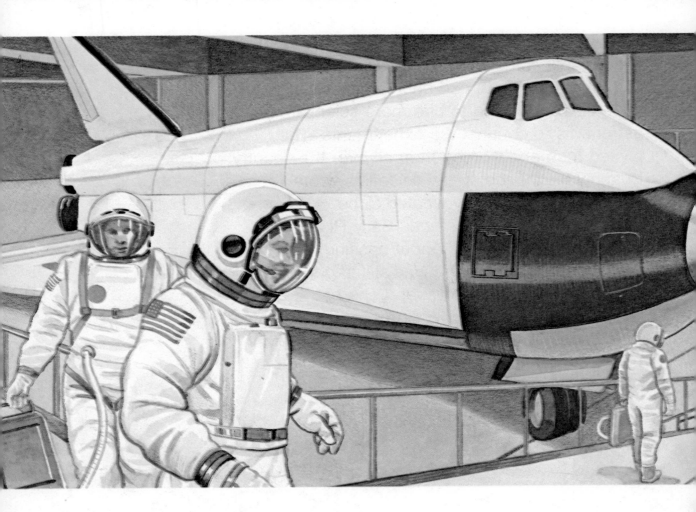

NASA kept Sally guessing for months before
they finally chose her as an astronaut.

These new astronauts will work on a space
shuttle that will carry them into space. The
space shuttle will be able to land on a runway
instead of splashing down in the ocean. This
means that the space shuttle can be refueled
and used over and over again like a jet. NASA
will be able to launch weekly space flights
instead of one or two a year.

Dr. Sally Ride will study at the Johnson
Space Center in Houston, Texas, for two years
before her first space flight. "I became an
astronaut for one reason," she said. "I am
fascinated by outer space. I always have been.
Besides, who could turn down the chance to go
up in space? Thirty years from now, when
they're selling round-trip tickets to Mars,
it might not be as exciting, but right now
it's a once-in-a-lifetime opportunity."

Comprehension Check

1. What did Sally Ride want to be before she became interested in the space program?
2. Why did Sally lose a very important tennis match?
3. How do you think Sally felt when she was chosen to be an astronaut?
4. How could Sally's training in tennis help her become an astronaut?
5. What kind of person do you think would make a good astronaut?

Skill Check

Is "Sally Ride: Scientist-Astronaut" fact or fiction? How do you know?

Read the three sentences below. Which sentences are fact? Check the facts in the selection you just read.

1. The space monster asked how to get to the top of the tall building.
2. Sally Ride helped pay her way through college by giving tennis lessons.
3. Sally Ride was chosen to conduct experiments on board the space shuttle.

The Elephant Trainer

by Duncan Searl

Rex cut the strings and the great red banner unfurled. Its painted letters glittered in the sun. Four children from town looked on.

"Dr. Szabo's Magical Animal Caravan and Daredevil Highwire Troupe," the older girl read aloud.

"What's a highwire troupe?" the little boy asked.

"You know," said the girl. "Acrobats, tightrope walkers, and all that."

"A magical caravan?" the boy asked.

"A traveling show with trained animals, I suppose," the older girl replied.

"Hey!" the boy called to Rex. "How many elephants are in your caravan?"

Rex hated that question. He pretended not to hear, but the boy asked again.

"No elephants," Rex called back. "But we do have lions, tigers, bears, trained ponies . . ."

"No elephants?" the boy said. "Some circus." And the four children walked away toward town.

It was almost show time. Soon Dr. Szabo, the ringmaster, would blow the whistle to start the show. Rex looked into the main tent and saw many empty seats. He shook his head and walked to the dressing tent to put on his clown costume.

In the tent Snappy, the other clown, was gluing on a big red nose. "Hurry up, Rex, you're late," he said.

"There are fewer than a hundred people out there tonight," Rex said. "I know it won't get better until we have some elephants. People expect elephants at a circus. With elephants we could have a parade through town and . . ."

A loud whistle interrupted Rex. The lights dimmed.

"Ladies and gentlemen! Children of all ages! A thousand welcomes to Dr. Szabo's Magical Animal Caravan and Daredevil Highwire Troupe."

Rex struggled into his baggy pants. Snappy brushed on Rex's makeup while Rex laced up his big, floppy shoes.

"I can hardly stand in these shoes," said Snappy.

"That's why I'd rather be an elephant trainer," said Rex.

Lady Tanya was already in the ring. Her four white ponies were dancing on their hind legs. It was Rex's job to hold the hoop that each pony jumped through to end the act.

Rex grabbed the hoop and ran into the ring. As he ran, he tripped over his shoes and fell on his face. The crowd roared with laughter.

The rest of the show went very well. Snappy made everyone laugh with his baby carriages, buckets of mud, and funny trombone. Another performer made three lions roar and paw angrily before they rolled on the barrels. Some bears rode their skateboards up and down ramps and played the drums. Two seals balanced beachballs, clapped their flippers, and waddled in time to the music. Rex's mother and father performed their highwire bicycle act, and it was a big hit. The crowd applauded loudly.

Yes, the show went very well indeed. There was only one problem. There were no elephants.

The next day Rex wandered into the empty tent. He saw Dr. Szabo talking to Tanya.

"Rex," Dr. Szabo called, "your clowning is getting better. Your opening fall looked good."

"It was real," said Rex, "but it didn't feel so good. Dr. Szabo, this caravan needs something."

"It needs a lot of things," said Dr. Szabo.

"Most of all, it needs elephants," said Rex.

"Elephants!" shouted Dr. Szabo. "Do you know how much elephants cost? Do you know how much it costs to feed and train them?"

"I can train them. Elephants are smart."

"You?" Dr. Szabo laughed. "Just forget it, Rex. Why, if someone gave me two elephants tomorrow, I wouldn't take them. Where would I put them? No, it's out of the question."

Rex walked back to his trailer. His mother and father were cooking dinner.

"How's your juggling coming along?" his father asked.

"Elephants," said Rex.

"You can't juggle elephants," his father said. "Besides, we don't have any."

"That's the problem," said Rex. "We need elephants. I could train them. Elephants never forget anything."

"Unlike someone I know," said his mother, "who forgets to study every day, even though he promised to study if we let him travel with us."

The next morning Rex saw Dr. Szabo talking excitedly with several people.

"You won't believe this," said Dr. Szabo. "A dear friend of mine has sold his circus in Spain, but he cannot bear to sell his elephants, Don and Carlos. They are so smart and well trained, they are like children to him. So he has decided to give them to our caravan. Why, only yesterday I was saying how much we need elephants."

"*I* was saying that," Rex interrupted. "You said you wouldn't take elephants even if . . ."

"No, no, I've always loved elephants," said Dr. Szabo. "They are noble, intelligent animals. You may not know this, Rex, but people expect to see elephants. I don't know how we have managed without them for so long."

Weeks later the elephants arrived. They came in a cattle truck with two drivers.

"These elephants are trouble," one driver said.

"Stupid!" the other exclaimed.

"What?" said Dr. Szabo. "They should be smart and well trained. Here, let me show you. Come down, Carlos. Move along, Don," he called. But the elephants wouldn't move.

Next Rex tried. "Come here, fellow. That a boy." But the elephants just stared at him. He clapped his hands several times. That didn't do any good either. In the end it took twelve people to push and pull the elephants into the animal tent.

Dr. Szabo was angry. He turned to Rex. "OK, big Mr. Elephant Trainer, so you think elephants are smart? You train them."

40

All day long Rex worked with the elephants.
But no matter what he did, Don and Carlos would
not move. Rex couldn't make the animals sit
down. They wouldn't even walk. Don and Carlos
just looked at him sadly.

The next day Rex tried again. And the next
day. A week passed. Still nothing changed.
Dr. Szabo said he would have to sell the
elephants to a zoo.

Rex spent more and more time with the
elephants. He slept near them. He ate his meals
in their tent. He even studied next to them.

One day, after spending four hours with Don and Carlos, Rex was ready to give up. He sat back in the hay, picked up a book, and started to read. It was his Spanish book.

"How are you? *¿Cómo está usted?*" he read aloud. Don shifted in his stall. Carlos picked up his floppy ears. Rex continued to read.

"One, two, three. *Uno, dos, tres.*" Suddenly Don was stamping his feet. First one time, then twice, and finally three times.

"Four. *Cuatro,*" Rex read. Don stamped four times. Then Carlos stood up and stamped four times too. Rex couldn't believe it. He started turning the pages of the book wildly.

42

"Lie down! ¡*Acuéstate!*" he read. Immediately the elephants lay in the hay.

"Pick me up! ¡*Cárgame!*" he ordered. Don circled his trunk around Rex and swung him up into the air.

"Elephants who understand Spanish!" Rex shouted. "Of course!"

Rex learned more Spanish that day than he had all year. It didn't take long before he had his act together. He called the caravan members together to see it.

"Such intelligent animals," said Dr. Szabo. "I always knew Rex was a natural trainer."

"That boy can sure juggle those elephants," said Rex's father.

"I'm glad that Rex is studying his Spanish," said Rex's mother with a smile.

Comprehension Check

1. What kind of animal did Rex think the circus needed?
2. When Rex performed before the audience, what kind of costume did he wear?
3. Why did Rex think it was important for a circus to have elephants?
4. Why was Dr. Szabo angry after the elephants arrived?
5. How did Rex finally get the elephants to understand him?
6. Have you ever trained an animal or would you like to? What kinds of things would you teach it to do?

Skill Check

How are the vowel sounds in the words in each of these rows alike?

1. red	big	trunk	stamp
2. for	start	first	furl
3. hate	time	face	nose
4. mud	pants	job	shift
5. smart	girl	hard	her

Mystery Words

Sometimes as you read, you may see a word that you just can't figure out. You can use the meaning of the sentence as a clue to help you figure out a word you don't know. Read this sentence.

We have b_____ in our classroom.

What words might make sense in the sentence? The consonant b tells you the word must begin with the sound the letter b stands for. Did the words you chose begin with b?

Here is another sentence with a mystery word.

I love to watch the p_____t in Ernie's pet shop.

What word might make sense in the sentence? Look at the consonants p and t. They tell you something about the word. The word must begin with the sound the letter p stands for. It must end with the sound the letter t stands for.

Here is another consonant clue.

I love to watch the p__rr__t in Ernie's pet shop.

Now what do you think the mystery word is?
1. How can the words in a sentence help you figure out a word you don't know?
2. How can looking at the consonants help you figure out a mystery word?

Practice

Which of the three words below each sentence belongs in the blank? Use the meaning of each sentence and the consonants as clues.
1. Every night Lisa watches the stars from her g_____.
   a. golden   b. garden   c. window
2. She dreams of taking a trip in a r_____t.
   a. rabbit   b. jet   c. rocket
3. The night is dark, but the stars are bright s_____r.
   a. silver   b. gold   c. supper

4. The moon looks b__gg__r than the stars around it.
   a. beggar   b. bigger   c. lighter
5. At n_____t, it's hard to see the clouds.
   a. night   b. nest   c. dusk

`Use sentence meanings and consonants to help you figure out any unfamiliar words in the story "Pecos Bill Rides a Tornado."

Pecos Bill Rides a Tornado

by W. Blassingame

There's a horse named Widow-Maker
And he can't be rode.
Every cowboy that tries
Is sure to be throwed.

That's the way the song was at first. Texas
cowboys sang it while they tended their herds.
Then one starry night a cowboy named Pecos Bill
came riding through the country. He heard
the song, and he started to laugh. "You've got
that wrong," he told the other cowboys. Bill
leaned back in his saddle and sang:
"There's not a horse that can't be rode,
Because I'm a cowboy who can't be
throwed."

48

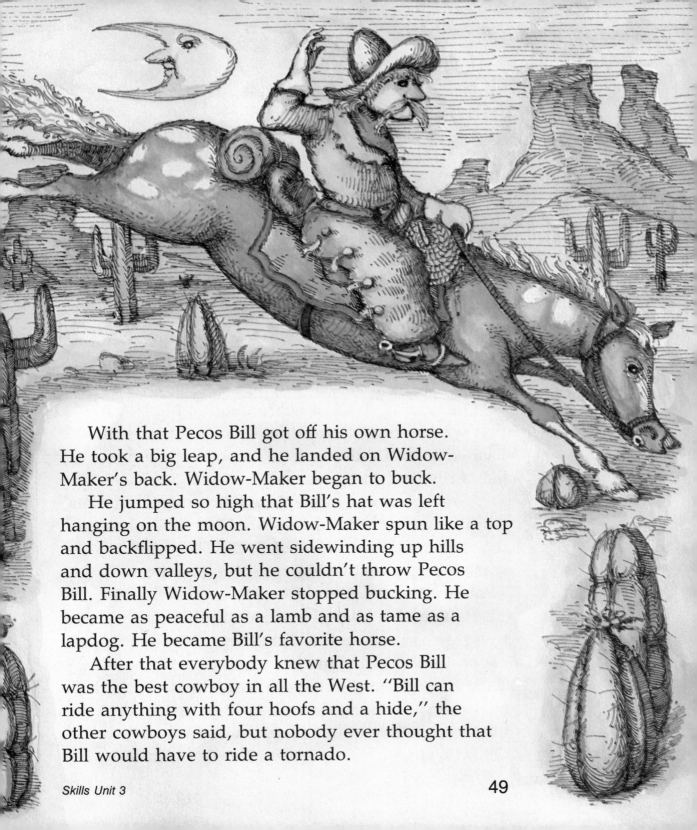

With that Pecos Bill got off his own horse. He took a big leap, and he landed on Widow-Maker's back. Widow-Maker began to buck.

He jumped so high that Bill's hat was left hanging on the moon. Widow-Maker spun like a top and backflipped. He went sidewinding up hills and down valleys, but he couldn't throw Pecos Bill. Finally Widow-Maker stopped bucking. He became as peaceful as a lamb and as tame as a lapdog. He became Bill's favorite horse.

After that everybody knew that Pecos Bill was the best cowboy in all the West. "Bill can ride anything with four hoofs and a hide," the other cowboys said, but nobody ever thought that Bill would have to ride a tornado.

This is the way that it happened.

One spring day Bill heard about a big storm that was roaring in from the west. Lightning flashed and thunder rolled. The rain came down like a river standing on end.

Now about that same time Bill watched another storm come up from the south. The wind blew one thousand and two miles an hour. The lightning was so bright that cowboys all the way from Texas to Wyoming could see it.

Halfway between the West and the South, these two storms ran together. They met head on. They began to chase one another around and around. They turned into the biggest tornado anybody had ever seen. The tornado was so high its top kept pushing the sky out of place. Its bottom dug the Grand Canyon.

50

This tornado kept on roaring and leapfrogging all over the West. Bill heard that it picked up a thousand head of cattle on the Heart Bar Ranch in Texas. It put them down nice as you please on the Crooked S Ranch in Arizona.

Then it picked up the cattle on the Crooked S and put them down on the Bent W Ranch in Kansas. It picked up the state of Oklahoma and put it down in New Mexico. Then it put New Mexico where Oklahoma had been.

All this was bad enough, but then the tornado made a mistake. It came roaring up the Pecos River in Texas, right past Pecos Bill's house.

Pecos Bill wasn't home when the tornado passed. He was driving some cattle to market, but he soon came riding back. "Whoa, Widow-Maker!" Pecos Bill shouted. He stopped to look around.

There stood Slue-Foot Sue, Bill's wife, but there wasn't any ranchhouse. There wasn't any barn. There weren't any cottonwood trees along the Pecos River. There wasn't even any Pecos River.

"Sue," Bill shouted, "what has happened around here? Where's our Pecos River?"

"The tornado took it," said Sue.

"Where's our house and barn and cottonwood trees?" Bill asked.

"The tornado took them too," Sue said.

That made Pecos Bill mad. "I've been driving cattle for a long time," he said. "I'm hungry. Now I come home, and some crazy tornado has stolen my house—the kitchen and all. Which way did it go?"

52

"That way," Sue said, pointing west, "but you can't catch it. It was traveling a thousand and two miles an hour."

"Well, it better not let me catch it," Bill said. "No tornado is going to take my house and get away with it. Get up, Widow-Maker!"

Bill galloped west. He rushed straight across Texas. He was racing over the mountains when he ran into a twenty-foot rattlesnake. The snake stood on its tail to block the way.

"You're in a mighty big hurry," the rattlesnake said.

Pecos Bill was surprised to hear a rattlesnake talk, but he was in too big a hurry to ask about it. "Did you see a tornado come past here?" he asked the snake. "It was carrying a house and a barn and some cottonwood trees and the Pecos River."

"I did," the rattlesnake said.

"Which way did it go?"

"I won't tell, unless you can make me," the rattlesnake said. "I'm twenty feet long. I'm mean, and I'm bad, and I'm ready to fight."

Pecos Bill got down from Widow-Maker's back. "All right," he said. "I'm in a hurry. So to make it a fair fight, I'll give you the first three bites."

The rattlesnake bit Pecos Bill once. It turned gray and began to look sick.

It bit Bill again, and it turned green. The rattles on its tail started to fall off. "That's enough," the rattlesnake said. "I don't want to fight." It pointed its head toward the north. "Your tornado went that way."

Bill jumped on Widow-Maker and galloped north. They rushed over more mountains and more prairies. They were racing through some high mountains when Bill looked up. He saw the tornado rushing toward them. It was leapfrogging from one mountain to another, turning them upside down. It was turning rivers around so they would run upstream. Lightning was flashing in eighty-two directions.

Quickly Bill took his lasso and began to spin it around and around his head. It was the longest lasso in the world. The noose got bigger and bigger, and the line got longer and longer as Bill swung it.

Then he let the noose go. It went up and up. It slipped along the bottom of the sky and over the top of the tornado.

Not even Pecos Bill could stop that tornado, but he held onto his lasso. It pulled him high in the air. It swung him back and forth like the tail of a kite.

This didn't worry Bill. Hand over hand, he climbed up the lasso. He swung himself on the tornado's back. He began to ride it like a wild horse.

"Whoopee!" Bill yelled, waving his hat with one hand. "Buck, you crazy tornado!"

Well, that tornado really went wild. It backflipped and turned head over heels. It went sidewinding over mountains and down valleys. It sent lightning off in one hundred and eighty-two directions, but it couldn't throw Pecos Bill.

Bill sat there, hitting the tornado with his hat and kicking it with his heels. Then he began to sing:

"This tornado doesn't want to be rode,
But Old Pecos Bill, he can't be throwed."

Finally the tornado began to get tired. It got weaker and weaker. Bill made it put the cattle from the Heart Bar and the Crooked S and the Bent W ranches back where they came from.

He made it put Oklahoma back below Kansas and New Mexico back next to Arizona. Then he made it carry his house and his barn and the cottonwood trees and the Pecos River back to Texas.

By now the tornado was tired. It just had strength for one last bolt of lightning. Bill grabbed the lightning bolt and slid down it to the ground.

Slue-Foot Sue and Widow-Maker were waiting in front of the house. "You've got our house and barn back," Sue said, "but what took you so long?"

58

"Sue," Pecos Bill said, "I've been fighting
with a rattlesnake and I've been riding the
tornado from Oklahoma to New Mexico to Texas.
Now I'm too tired and hungry to answer
questions."

They went inside to have supper. While they
were eating, Sue heard a noise outside. "What's
that?" she asked Pecos Bill.

Bill looked out the window. "It's that
tornado," he said, "but now it's settled down
to no more than a spring breeze. It's playing
in our yard like a puppy."

"Well, let's keep it," Sue said. "It'll be
nice to have a breeze of our own when the
weather gets hot this summer."

Comprehension Check

1. Who was Widow-Maker?
2. What did the tornado do at the Heart Bar Ranch in Texas?
3. Why was Pecos Bill angry when he got home?
4. What happened to the rattlesnake that bit Pecos Bill?
5. Do you think the events in this story could have happened? Why or why not?
6. Have you ever been caught in a bad storm? What did you do?

Skill Check

Which of the three words below each sentence belongs in the blank? Use the meaning of each sentence and the consonants as clues.

1. Pecos Bill tamed a wild h_____.
   a. hill   b. horse   c. cow
2. The tornado took a thousand head of c_____.
   a. cattle   b. cookies   c. lightning
3. A rattlesnake b___t Pecos Bill.
   a. bought   b. bit   c. liked
4. Pecos Bill galloped across the state of T__x__s.
   a. Oklahoma   b. taxes   c. Texas

Delilah

by Carole Hart

> These two stories are about a
> character named Delilah. By reading
> the stories, you will find out what
> kinds of things Delilah likes to do.

Birthday

It was two weeks before her birthday. Delilah
wanted a record player, but the trick was to let
her mother and father know without really
telling them. If she told them, it wouldn't be a
surprise. And she knew her mother and father loved to
surprise her. At dinner that night she dropped
a hint to them.

"We're studying how sound works at school,"
she said. "I learned how you get sound out of a
record player. It's very, very interesting."

Several nights later they all went shopping together. Delilah stopped at a record bin and began thumbing through it.

Her mother said, "We'll meet you in Housewares." She left Delilah thumbing.

A salesclerk came over. "May I help you?" he asked Delilah.

"Just looking," Delilah said, and made her way to Housewares, where she found her mother and father buying garbage bags.

In the car on the way home, Delilah asked her father what his favorite kind of music was.

"I like all kinds," he said.

"I guess I like rock best," her mother said.

"Me too," said Delilah.

"OK. I get it," her father said. Then he turned the car radio to a rock station. Delilah wasn't so sure her father understood her hint.

62

The next week she borrowed the record of
<u>Peter and the Wolf</u> from the library.

"Why did you take out a record?" her mother
asked.

"Because I like it," Delilah answered. "And
I'm going over to Monica's house to listen to
it."

"Too bad you don't have your own record
player," her mother said. "By the way, would you
mind picking up a carton of milk on your way
home?"

Delilah didn't mind at all. In fact, she was
very happy. She was sure her mother had guessed
what she wanted for her birthday. Now all she
had to do was wait, which was very hard to do.

But finally her birthday arrived. She got seven out of ten wrong on a spelling test because she couldn't pay attention. Then her teacher asked her a question she couldn't answer because she didn't hear it.

It would have been an awful day, except that it was her birthday. When Delilah got home from school, her mother and father were waiting for her. They had both come home early from work.

"Happy birthday, Delilah!" they said at the same time.

"Thank you," Delilah said, biting her lip. She could hardly stand the suspense.

"We have a present for you," her father said. "It's in your room."

Delilah dashed off to her room. When she got there, she stopped short. She was very surprised. Curled up on her bed was a puppy. It was sleeping peacefully.

"Oh!" Delilah said.

The puppy opened its eyes and looked at her without raising its head. Delilah loved the little dog at once and forever. She called her puppy Hi-Fido.

Sing for Joy

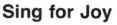

On the first day of spring, it was beautiful. It made Delilah happy. It made her so happy that she wanted to sing.

"Oh, what a beautiful morning," she sang as she put on her favorite pair of jeans.

Her mother came rushing in from the kitchen. "Delilah, what's wrong?" she asked.

"Nothing," Delilah answered. "It's a beautiful day, and I was just singing about it."

"So that's what it was. I thought you were in pain."

Delilah blushed.

"Delilah, I know it's not right for a mother to be discouraging, but you are the worst singer I've ever heard. If you must sing, please sing somewhere else. OK?"

"Somewhere else." Delilah sang the words sweetly.

"That's a very old joke," her mother said, but she laughed anyway.

Delilah went out for a walk. It was a beautiful day. It made Delilah happy. It made her so happy that, once again, she burst into song.

A police officer, passing in his car, screeched to a stop. "What's the matter?" he asked.

"Nothing," Delilah answered. "It's a beautiful day, and I was just singing about it."

"So that's what it was. It sounded like appendicitis!"

Delilah blushed.

"I don't know how to say this to you, but you're the worst singer I ever heard. Your singing is terrible," he said.

"So I've been told," Delilah answered. "Sorry if I scared you."

"That's OK. But if I were you, I wouldn't sing anymore. Especially in public. So long." And he took off.

It was still a beautiful day, but Delilah wasn't happy anymore. She wandered into the park and found a bench where she could sit and feel sorry for herself.

After a while she heard a faraway sound. It was band music. Awful band music. The worst band music she had ever heard. She followed the sound.

Soon she arrived at a small band shell, occupied by a small band. There were six players, playing a tambourine, a drum, a cornet, a trombone, and two tubas. And there was a bandleader.

68

"Hi!" Delilah said when they'd finished their number.

"What did you say?" the bandleader asked her.

Delilah moved a little closer. "I said hi. Can you play 'When the Saints Go Marchin' In'?" she asked.

"Sure," the bandleader said.

"Would you?" she asked.

"Of course," the bandleader said happily. It was the first time he'd ever been asked to play anything except "somewhere else."

Delilah climbed onto the band shell.

"A-one, a-two, a-three, a-four," the bandleader counted.

And the band played. And Delilah sang. When they finished, they all clapped for each other.

"Do you know 'Hail, Hail, the Gang's All Here'?" Delilah asked.

"Sure do," said the bandleader.

And, on the first day of spring, Delilah sang for joy.

Comprehension Check

1. In the story "Birthday," what kind of present did Delilah want?
2. Do you think Delilah's parents knew what she wanted for her birthday? Why or why not?
3. What hints did Delilah drop about what she wanted for her birthday? What else could she have done?
4. In the story "Sing for Joy," what made Delilah want to sing?
5. Why did Delilah's mother ask her to sing somewhere else?
6. Why did the police officer stop and ask Delilah if anything was wrong?
7. Do you like to sing? What are some of your favorite songs?

Tuesday I Was Ten

by Kaye Starbird

Tuesday I was ten, and though
The fact delights me plenty,
It sort of startles me to know
I'm now a half of twenty.

It's nice to own a bigger bike
With brakes along the wheels
And figure skates (the kind I like)
And shoes with little heels,
And have a real allowance too,
To make me wise and thrifty;
But still, I can't believe (can you?)
I'm now a fifth of fifty!

Although an age like ten appears
Quite young and un-adventure-y,
My gosh! In only ninety years
My age will be a century!

How Is a Table Like You?

by Cynthia Basil

What does a table have that you have?

Legs! A table stands on four legs. You stand on two legs.

Some table legs end with feet. Your legs end with feet.

What has elbows but no arms?

The pipes in the kitchen. Elbow is the name for the part of a pipe with a bend.

Some macaroni has a bend too. It is called elbow macaroni.

What do your head and a clock have in front?

74

A face! What else does a clock have that you
have? Two hands. A clock's hands point to the
time on its face. Your hands can point anywhere.

A clock's face has no eyes, no nose, and no
mouth. But your face has all of these.

A potato has eyes but no face. A potato's eyes
can't see. Your eyes can.

What has a mouth but no face?

A bottle! A bottle's mouth is an opening for things to go in and come out. Your mouth is an opening. Food can go in and talk can come out.

A cave has a mouth too. A cave's mouth is an opening in a hill. A cave's mouth can't open and close. Your mouth can.

What does your mouth have inside that a comb and a saw have?

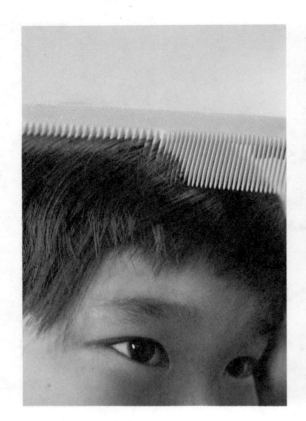
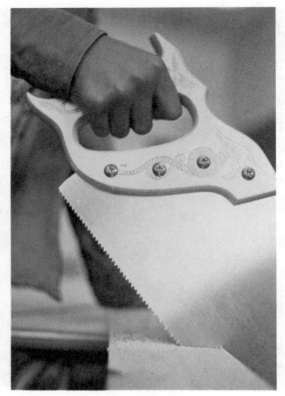

Teeth! A comb's teeth and a saw's teeth are in
a row. Your teeth are in a row.

Most combs and saws have only one row of teeth.
You have two rows.

A saw's teeth can cut wood. Your teeth cut food.

An airplane doesn't have teeth, but what else
does it have that you have?

A nose and a belly! If you could fly, your nose and belly would be where an airplane's nose and belly are.

A road has something that you have too. What is it?

 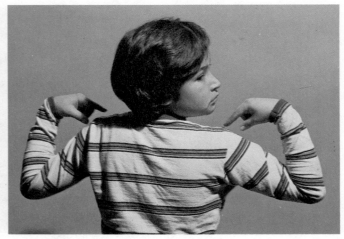

Shoulders! A road's shoulders are at its sides.
Your shoulders are at the sides of your neck.

What does a car have that you have?

A body!

A car's\body and your body are made of many
different parts and they have different names.
Parts of some things and parts of you have the
same names because in some ways they are alike.
But nothing is exactly like you!

80

Comprehension Check

1. What is the part of a pipe with a bend called?
2. What does a clock have that you also have?
3. How are your face and a clock's face different?
4. How are you and an airplane alike? How are you and an airplane different?
5. Can you think of anything else that is like you?

Skill Check

Read each sentence. Then answer the question that follows.

The plumber went into the kitchen and checked the elbow.
1. In this sentence the word elbow means
   a. part of a person's arm
   b. the part of a pipe with a bend

He banged his elbow.
2. In this sentence the word elbow means
   a. part of a person's arm
   b. the part of a pipe with a bend

The car pulled off onto the shoulder.
3. In this sentence the word shoulder means
   a. part of a person's body
   b. the side of the road

She threw her coat over her shoulder.
4. In this sentence the word shoulder means
   a. part of a person's body
   b. the side of the road

Dictionary and Glossary

A dictionary or a glossary is a wonderful tool. It can help you learn what words mean.

Guide words are found on top of a dictionary or glossary page. They help you find the word you want. **Guide words** are the first and last words on the page. You have to check to see that the word you are looking for comes alphabetically between the two guide words on the top of the page. If it does, then your word can be found on that page.

Guide Words

Entry Word

42   bald eagle ꟷ balsa

bald eagle, a large, powerful, North American eagle with white feathers on its head, neck, and tail. See picture.

bale (bāl), **1** a large bundle of material securely wrapped or bound for shipping or storage: *a bale of cotton.* **2** make into bales: *We saw a big machine bale hay.* 1 *noun,* 2 *verb,* **baled, bal ing.**

bale ful (bāl′fəl), threatening; hostile: *The librarian gave the noisy children a baleful look. adjective.*

bald eagle—about 3 feet (1 meter) from head to tail

Definition

A dictionary or glossary has entry words and information about each word. The **entry word** is the word you are looking up. Each entry word is listed in alphabetical order and has one definition or more. The **definition** tells you what the entry word means.

An entry word and the information about it is called an **entry.** An entry may also have a picture.

82

Sometimes an entry has a sentence that uses the entry word. The sentence may be printed in special type. The sentence will help you understand what the word means.

Look at the entry for the word desire.

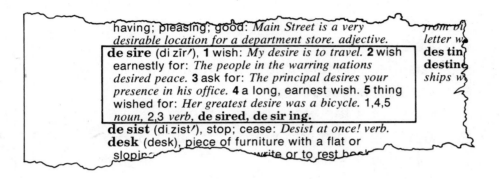

having; pleasing; good: *Main Street is a very desirable location for a department store. adjective.*

de sire (di zīr′), **1** wish: *My desire is to travel.* **2** wish earnestly for: *The people in the warring nations desired peace.* **3** ask for: *The principal desires your presence in his office.* **4** a long, earnest wish. **5** thing wished for: *Her greatest desire was a bicycle.* 1,4,5 *noun*, 2,3 *verb*, **de sired, de sir ing.**

de sist (di zist′), stop; cease: *Desist at once! verb.*
desk (desk), piece of furniture with a flat or sloping

The first sentence in the entry for desire is: My desire is to travel. What other sentences are given?

When you look up the meaning of a new word, be sure to look for sentences that show how the word may be used.

Many times a word with a special ending will not have its own entry in the dictionary or glossary. To find the meaning of a word that has an ending added to it, you need to look up the **root word.**

Look at the entry desire. Look at the two words printed in dark print at the end of the entry. These words, desired and desiring, show different endings for the root word desire. If you wanted to find desired or desiring, you would need to look up the root word desire.

1. What can the sentences in a definition tell you?
2. When a word has a special ending, what part of the word should you look up?
3. If you wanted to find the meaning of the word crinkled, what word would you look up?

Practice

Use the glossary in the back of this book to answer these questions:
1. What does the word plume mean?
2. What are the guide words on page 336 of your glossary?
3. What two special endings does the word blur have?
4. If you wanted to find the word rumbled in the glossary, what word would you have to look up?

Use the glossary at the back of this book to find the meaning of the words you don't know in the story "An Island Is Born."

An Island Is Born

by Duncan Searl

The island of Surtsey was formed
in 1963. In 1965 the government of Iceland
made the island a nature reserve
and bird sanctuary. This is a story
about how it came to be.

It was six o'clock in the morning, and Arni
had already been working for several hours. Now
the fishing lines were finally in place. Arni
and his father, Captain Tomasson, watched the
gray sea. In the distance was the western shore
of Iceland.

"You can see the Westman Islands," Captain
Tomasson said, pointing to a group of low-lying
black islands half hidden by clouds.

"But I can't see Heimaey," said Arni. Heimaey
was the island where they lived. "Is something
burning?" he asked. "I smell smoke."

"Maybe Olafur is burning the toast," his father replied. "Let's go see. I'm hungry."

Father and son went below for breakfast and a nap.

One hour later Arni was wakened by a shout. "Captain Tomasson! Come here at once!"

Arni raced to the deck, meeting his father on the way.

Olafur Vestmann was on watch when he smelled the smoke. Then, far off in the distance, he saw a large smoking object.

"So much black smoke," he said aloud. "Must be a burning ship." And so he called the captain.

Captain Tomasson steered toward the smoke. The sea grew rougher and rougher as they approached it. When they were a half mile from the smoke, the waves were so high they could go no farther safely. Arni looked at the smoke through his binoculars. But he couldn't believe what he saw.

Huge columns of ash and smoke were rising out of the sea. Great chunks of stone were being hurled into the air. A giant plume of white and black smoke billowed high into the sky. Within minutes this smoke was a mile high. A heavy rumbling beneath the sea shook the boat. Ashes were everywhere, and bright lightning made Arni shiver.

"We're sitting on top of a volcano," Captain
Tomasson shouted as he turned the wheel. "And
it's just beginning to erupt!"

The eruptions became more powerful as the
little boat steamed away from the volcano. By
the time the boat reached Heimaey, the plume of
smoke was over five miles high. All over Iceland
people saw the smoke as it caught the rays of
the setting sun.

The next morning Arni ran to the beach. The
smoke was still there, as high as ever.
Fountains of ash were still rocketing into the
sky. But something was different. Beneath the
plume of smoke was an island. An island that
had never been there before.

88

The island grew quickly. In four days it was 2,000 feet long and 200 feet high. The volcano continued to erupt. In two weeks the new island was bigger than all the other Westman Islands except Heimaey. The island was named Surtsey. And news of Surtsey spread quickly.

"Arni, will you come out on the boat with me tomorrow?" Captain Tomasson asked.

"Of course," said Arni. He hadn't been on his father's boat for several months. "Will there be any fish?" Arni asked. The volcano had driven most of the fish away. The fishermen of the Westman Islands were still waiting for the fish to return.

"No, there won't be any fish," said Captain Tomasson, "but there is a surprise. A group of scientists—geologists—want us to take them to Surtsey. They have come from the United States to study this volcano."

The next morning Arni helped the scientists carry their equipment aboard. Once the boat was in open water, Arni began asking questions.

"Why did the volcano erupt here?" he asked one of the scientists.

"The earth's crust," she explained, "is made up of huge sections of rock called *plates*. Sometimes these plates move. Iceland is above two plates that are pulling apart.

"Deep within the earth," she continued, "there is a great deal of burning, molten rock called *magma*. Magma can spill out through the space where the plates have pulled apart. We call that a *volcano*. Once the magma is out, it is called *lava*.

"The lava cools and hardens to form a mountain. More and more lava keeps spilling out through a hole called a *crater* in the middle of the mountain. Your new island, Surtsey, is the top of a mountain."

They were close enough to see Surtsey now. The volcano was still.

"Why did it stop erupting?" asked Arni.

"After a while the crater fills with rock and ash," she answered. "No more lava can get through."

"Look!" shouted Arni. "Birds are living on Surtsey. And there is even some grass growing there."

"You're right," said another scientist. "It doesn't take very long for normal life to begin on a volcanic island."

"Normal life," said Captain Tomasson. "That sounds good to me. Maybe now our lives will get back to normal too, and we can catch some fish."

Comprehension Check

1. On what island did Arni and his father live?
2. What caused all the smoke that Arni saw from his father's boat?
3. Why do you think Arni's father turned the boat away from the volcano?
4. Do you think that Arni was interested in finding out more about the volcano? Why do you think as you do?
5. Where would you look if you wanted to find out more information about volcanoes?

Skill Check

Read the following words. Then answer the questions below.

billowed   rocketing
erupting   steered

1. What root word must you look up to find the meaning of each word listed above?
2. Find each word in the glossary at the back of your book. On what page can each word be found? What are the guide words at the top of each of these pages?
3. What is the meaning of each word?
4. Make up a sentence using each word.

Somebody Stole Second

by Louise Munro Foley

"It's GONE!" Pete yelled. He stopped running. Scooter stopped throwing and Jenny ran in from left field.

Pete was right. It *was* gone. Second base had disappeared.

"Fine thing," said Pete. Pete was captain of the Jets. "First time this year that I hit a double and when I get here, second base is gone."

"Somebody stole second!" yelled Scooter as he jumped up and down. "Somebody stole second!" He poked Pete in the ribs. "Just like the Giants," yelled Scooter. "Somebody stole second!"

"BE QUIET, SCOOTER!" yelled Pete. "When the Giants steal second, it's GOOD. THIS . . . IS BAD."

"Yes," said Jenny slowly. "Somebody *really* stole second. They came along and carted it away."

The three children stared at the dirt where second base used to be. "Well, we still have first," said Jenny. She was looking over at the orange towel they used for first base.

"And THIRD!" yelled Scooter. He ran down to check the old piece of green carpet.

"But NO SECOND," said Pete.

Second base was an old red-and-black car cushion. Or at least it was before it disappeared. Pete's Mom used to sit on it when she was driving the car.

One day Pete's father brought home a new car
cushion, so they put the old cushion in Abner's
doghouse.

Abner was Pete's dog. He was a funny dog.
He didn't like dog food. He didn't like dog
biscuits. He liked graham crackers (with butter
and honey). And he didn't like doghouses. He liked
Pete's bedroom.

So, when the Jets needed a second base, Pete
took Abner's red-and-black car cushion. Abner
never slept in the doghouse anyway. He slept in
Pete's bedroom.

Every night Abner would jump into bed with
Pete. Pete had a nice soft bed with a nice big
pillow. Pete would snuggle down beside Abner and
hug his pillow and go to sleep.

So Abner didn't really need the doghouse or the car cushion. He had Pete's bed to sleep in. And that was how the car cushion became second base.

Scooter sat down in the dirt. "How can we play the Stars without a second base?" he asked.

The Stars and the Jets were rivals. They had a big game coming up the next day. It was a play-off.

"We can't," said Pete. "It's against the rules to play without a second base."

"We have to find it," said Jenny.

"Well, it didn't get up and walk away," said Scooter. "Somebody STOLE it."

"Hey!" yelled Jenny. "Who are our enemies?"

"The Stars!" yelled Pete.

"Then let's go!" yelled Jenny.

The Jets went looking for the Stars. The
Stars were practicing for the big game.

"Keep your eyes open," whispered Pete. "Maybe
we'll spot it."

The Stars were good ball players. They had
four players. They had two catcher's mitts. And
they had a second base. But it wasn't the Jets'
red-and-black car cushion. It was a dirty potato
sack.

"I don't see it," said Pete. "Let's go."

The children spent all day looking for second
base. They asked a lot of people. They asked a
lot of kids. They looked in a lot of funny
places like the garage, the washing machine, and
the baby's sandbox.

But they didn't find second base. They looked
for a long time. Then Pete had another idea.

"Maybe," he said, "just MAYBE Abner borrowed his pillow back."

They ran out and looked in the doghouse. It was dark inside. Pete crawled in. It was smelly. "It's dark in here," he yelled. His voice sounded funny. He was holding his nose. Scooter lent him his flashlight.

"Nope!" Pete yelled. "No second base!" He backed out of Abner's doghouse.

"No second base . . . no play-off tomorrow," said Scooter sadly.

"I'm tired of looking," said Jenny.

"Me too," said Pete. "Let's go inside."

Pete's mother gave them each a glass of milk. Then they went upstairs to Pete's room to read. Pete and Jenny flopped out on the floor. Scooter flopped out on the bed. He wiggled. He squirmed. He rolled over. Then he looked at Pete and said, "You have a lumpy bed."

"I have a nice bed!" yelled Pete crossly.

"Lumpy!" yelled Scooter. He pounded the bed with his fist. "A great big lump, right here!"

Pete was mad. He got up to look. Scooter was right. His bed *was* lumpy. "That's a new lump," said Pete. "I've never seen that lump before." He yanked down the bedspread.

"It's second base!" he yelled. They all looked. There it was . . . second base . . . right in the middle of Pete's bed.

"ABNER DID IT!" yelled Pete. "Abner wanted
a pillow!" He was laughing. They were all
laughing. "This is going TOO far!" said Pete.

"He can eat my graham crackers and he can
sleep in my room, BUT he'll just have to find
another pillow.

"Because NOBODY, not even ABNER, gets away
with stealing second base from the Jets!"

100

Comprehension Check

1. How did the children feel when they couldn't find second base?
2. What did the missing second base look like?
3. Why did Pete crawl into Abner's doghouse?
4. Where did the Jets find second base?
5. Do you think the Jets could have played baseball without their second base? What else could they have used?

Skill Check

The sentences below tell some of the events that happened in the story you just read. Put these events in the order in which they happened.

1. They found second base in the middle of Pete's bed.
2. They looked in the doghouse.
3. Somebody stole second.
4. The Jets went looking for the Stars.
5. They went upstairs to Pete's room.
6. The children looked in the garage, the washing machine, and the baby's sandbox.

Jack and the Beanstalk

Once upon a time there lived a woman who had a son named Jack. The woman and her son were very poor. All they had was a small house and a cow.

Jack and his mother worked long hours in their garden to grow food. But they never had enough to eat.

Jack's mother needed money to buy food and warm clothes. So one day she told Jack to take their cow to town and sell it. Jack went off to town with the cow.

On the way Jack met a man. The man said, "Good morning. Where are you going this fine day?"

"I'm going to town to sell this cow," Jack answered.

The man said, "I'll trade you some magic beans for your cow." The man held out his hand. He showed Jack some brightly colored beans.

The colors of the beans seemed to grow brighter as Jack looked at them. Jack really wanted the beans. So he gave away the cow and took the beans home.

When Jack's mother saw the beans she was very angry. She threw the beans out the window and sent Jack to bed without his supper.

The next morning Jack saw something growing outside his window. The magic beans had grown overnight into a huge beanstalk! It was so tall that Jack could not see the top of it.

Jack went out and started to climb the beanstalk. He climbed and climbed until he got to the top. And there before him, Jack saw a strange new land.

Jack started walking. Soon he came to a castle and knocked on the door. A woman opened the door.

"I'm hungry," said Jack. "May I have some bread?"

"Yes," said the woman. "But you must eat quickly. My husband is a mean giant. If he comes home and finds you, he'll eat you for dinner."

While Jack was eating, he heard a loud noise. The giant was coming home! Jack ran and hid in a basket. And just in time, for the giant was at the door!

As the giant came in, he sniffed and roared, "Fee, fi, fo, fum! I smell the blood of an Englishman!"

"That's just your dinner you smell," said the woman. "Sit down and eat."

So the giant ate his dinner. Then he got out a bag of gold coins and began to count them. After a while the giant fell asleep.

Jack had been watching the giant through a hole in the basket. Now Jack crawled out of the basket. He took the gold and quickly climbed down the beanstalk.

Jack's mother was very happy when she saw the gold. Now they would have money for food and clothes.

For the next week Jack helped his mother in the garden. Then he decided to climb the beanstalk again.

As before, Jack asked the woman for food. And, as before, she gave him something to eat. Jack ate the food quickly and hid in the basket.

Soon the giant came in and sniffed and roared, "Fee, fi, fo, fum! I smell the blood of an Englishman!"

"That's just your dinner you smell," said the woman. "Sit down and eat."

After the giant ate his dinner, he brought out a hen. He put the hen on the table, and it laid a golden egg. After a while the giant fell asleep.

Jack crawled out of the basket, took the hen, and climbed down the beanstalk.

Jack's mother was happy when she saw the hen lay golden eggs. Now they had enough gold for the rest of their lives.

Once again Jack worked in the garden for a week. Then he decided to climb the beanstalk again.

When he reached the top, the woman fed him again. Jack ate quickly and hid in the basket.

As soon as Jack had hidden, the giant came in the door. The giant sniffed and roared, "Fee, fi, fo, fum! I smell the blood of an Englishman!"

"That's just your dinner you smell," said the woman. "Sit down and eat."

After the giant had eaten his dinner, he took out a beautiful golden harp. He put it on the table. "Play," he said to the harp. The magic harp played a beautiful song, and soon the giant fell asleep.

Jack crawled out of the basket. He took the harp and started for the beanstalk. But suddenly the harp shouted, "Master! Master!"

The giant woke up and saw Jack. He ran after Jack. But just as he reached out to grab Jack, the giant tripped. Jack climbed down the beanstalk as fast as he could, yelling, "Mother! Mother! Bring the ax!" Jack could hear the giant coming down the beanstalk after him.

When Jack reached the bottom, his mother gave him an ax. Quickly Jack chopped down the beanstalk. It crashed to the ground. And that was the end of the giant.

Now Jack and his mother had everything they would ever need. They had their house and their garden. They had gold to buy food and clothes, a hen to lay golden eggs, and a harp to play songs for them. And so they lived happily ever after.

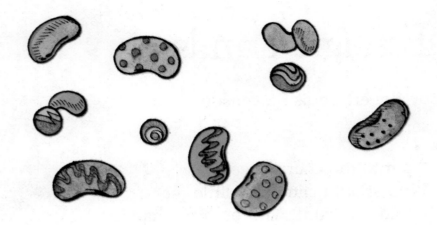

Comprehension Check

1. What did Jack do with the cow that he was supposed to sell?
2. Why do you think Jack's mother was angry when she saw the beans?
3. What kind of plant grew from the beans?
4. How do you think Jack felt when he saw the giant?
5. What did the harp do when Jack tried to take it?
6. Pretend that you found some magic beans and planted them. What would you like to see them grow to be?

Foreign Lands

by Robert Louis Stevenson

Up into the cherry tree
Who should climb but little me?
I held the trunk with both my hands
And looked abroad on foreign lands.

I saw the next door garden lie,
Adorned with flowers, before my eye,
And many pleasant places more
That I had never seen before.

I saw the dimpling river pass
And be the sky's blue looking-glass;
The dusty roads go up and down
With people tramping into town.

If I could find a higher tree
Farther and farther I should see,
To where the grown-up river slips
Into the sea among the ships.

To where the roads on either hand
Lean onward into fairy land,
Where all the children dine at five,
And all the playthings come alive.

Literary Unit

What Happened and Why?

Have you ever heard the silly old joke about the chicken? It goes like this: "Why did the chicken cross the road?" Can you guess the answer? Study the picture.

The chicken crossed the road because she wanted to get to the other side.

The sentence that gives the answer tells you two things. It tells you what the chicken did, and it tells you why she did it. The word because is a clue. It tells you that you are going to find out why something happened. Two other clue words that tell you why something happened are since and so.

The chicken walked slowly since the road was full of holes.

What happened? The chicken walked slowly. Why did the chicken walk slowly? The road was full of holes. What clue word did you use to help you find out why the chicken walked slowly?

Here is another sentence that tells what happened and why.

The chicken was tired so she stopped to rest.

What happened? The chicken stopped to rest. Why did the chicken stop to rest? She was tired. Did you use the clue word so to help you find out why the chicken stopped to rest?

114

Here is another sentence about the chicken that tells what happened and why. This sentence doesn't have a clue word to help you know why something happened, but you can still find the reason. First ask yourself, "What happened?" Find the answer in the sentence. Then ask, "Why did it happen?" The rest of the sentence will answer this question.

The chicken put on a hat to keep the sun out of her eyes.

What happened? The chicken put on a hat. Why did the chicken put on a hat? She put on a hat to keep the sun out of her eyes.

Practice

Read the sentences below. Decide what happened in each sentence. Then decide why it happened.

1. Roger closed the window because the room was cold.
2. People were wearing boots because the street was full of puddles.
3. The children could not play outside since the rain flooded the ground.
4. A dog sat under a tree to keep itself dry.
5. Mom and Dad built a fire so the house would be warmer.

When you read the next story, "The Private Eyes," look for sentences that tell why things happen.

The Private Eyes

by Laurel Dover

Raoul looked across the playground. He could see Noel and Wolf laughing and talking as they hurried away. Both boys wore blue jackets with the words "PRIVATE EYES" printed on the back. The Private Eyes was the name of a detective club. Raoul wished more than anything that he could be part of the club. But everything about the Private Eyes was a mystery, including how to get in.

Raoul watched as Wolf and Noel disappeared from sight. Then he slowly walked over to his bicycle. As soon as he got there, he spotted a piece of paper taped to its handlebars. He quickly peeled it off and began to read.

It said:

> Read this note, then get on your bike. Ride down Pine Street. Turn left on Van Dyck. Keep on riding until you see another note on the biggest oak tree.

"What kind of a joke is this?" thought Raoul. He started to tear it up. Then suddenly he changed his mind. He climbed onto his bike and took off. He couldn't help it. He was very curious.

He rode down Pine and turned onto Van Dyck Avenue. There were big oak trees everywhere. Then, all at once, he caught sight of the biggest tree of all. He sped toward it as fast as he could. Sure enough, tacked to one of its branches was another note. Raoul reached up and tore it off.

Skills Unit 7

Well done, Raoul, you're on your way.
Feel like solving a mystery today?
The next clue is under a soldier's feet.
Ride to find it, but stay on this street.

Raoul read and reread the note. "A soldier's feet? Now what in the world could that mean?" he asked aloud.

"How should I know!" answered a familiar voice. Raoul spun around. It was Sonia. She was in Raoul's class at school.

"Well, my father was a soldier once," the girl said, after Raoul had finished explaining. "And he lives on this street. But as far as I know, there aren't any notes under his feet."

"Come on, Sonia, be serious," said Raoul. "You've got to help me figure this out."

Sonia thought for a moment. "I've got it," she finally said. "The War Memorial is at the end of this street. And I know there's a statue of a soldier over there."

"Then what are we waiting for!" shouted Raoul. In a flash, the two children were off.

The statue was on a pedestal, and Sonia had to stretch to reach the soldier's feet. Taped under the soldier's boot was another mystery note. Sonia opened it and read it out loud.

From a soldier's feet to a wishing well
that stands beneath an iron bell.
You're doing fine, but there's more to go.
So hurry up and don't be slow.

"A wishing well?" said Raoul. "The only wishing well I can think of is five miles away."

"What about the old well behind the library?" suggested Sonia. "I've seen people throw pennies in there and make wishes."

"That's right," said Raoul. "And the fire station next door to it has a high belltower. Let's go!"

In minutes they had reached the library. They saw the old well and the bell. What they didn't see was the next note. They were just about to give up when they spotted Jill Litsky, a firefighter who worked at the fire station.

"Excuse me," Sonia called out to Jill. "Do you know of any other wishing wells in town?"

"What's all this interest in wells?" Jill
called back. "Are you going to write more crazy
poems like the one I found blowing down the
street before?" Jill reached into her pocket and
pulled out a piece of paper. "Here, listen to
this," she said, as she put on her glasses and
started to read.

Hope that your wishing well wish comes true.
But you still have to find another clue.
Two hundred new trucks all in a row.
The clue's on the wheel of one that's yellow.

Raoul and Sonia thought for a moment. There
was only one place in town where there were that
many new trucks—Reilly's Truck Sales. They
waved a quick good-by to Jill and hurried off.

When they got to the lot, they rode past
dozens of vans and pickups. But they couldn't
find one yellow truck.

"Hey, what do you kids want?" boomed a loud
voice. It was Big Jake Reilly.

"A yellow truck," Raoul answered.

"You're a little young to be a driver, aren't
you?" Jake chuckled. "Anyway, the only yellow
truck around here is mine."

"Can we see it?" Sonia asked excitedly.

"Sure, but I don't understand why," said Jake.

The kids followed him over to his truck. They
walked round and round it, until at last they
spied a tiny piece of paper taped to one of
its hubcaps. In a flash, they pulled it off.

"What's going on with you kids?" asked Jake. "Why all this interest in my truck? You sure are acting mysteriously."

"That's because everything's a mystery today," said Sonia, as she and Raoul jumped back on their bikes. They waved good-by to Big Jake Reilly. Then they rushed off.

When Raoul and Sonia reached the corner, they stopped to read their note. It said:

> Now circle back to your second clue.
> The number you want is two thirty-two.
> A barn's in the back, walk in if you dare.
> You'll find a surprise awaiting you there.

"What can it be?" cried Raoul. "I can't wait to find out!"

124

"Well, we'll have to," said Sonia. "We still have some detective work to do. We've got to figure out where you found that second clue."

"Under the soldier's boot," Raoul began. "No, wait," he corrected himself. "It was on the big oak tree right near your house."

"Two thirty-two Van Dyck Avenue," guessed Sonia. "I know where that is. In fact, I'm almost sure we know someone who lives there."

"Who?" Raoul wanted to know.

"That's just it," said Sonia. "I can't remember."

The two children rode down Van Dyck Avenue and turned up the driveway to number two thirty-two. In the back of the house they saw a big old garage that used to be a barn.

"This must be it," said Raoul. He and Sonia
walked into the barn and tiptoed up an old,
creaky stairway. At the top of the stairs
someone had painted a great big eye. An eerie
blue light was shining above it.

Sonia and Raoul were a little scared. Still,
they kept on going. At last they walked into
a large, dark room. As soon as they did, a light
went on.

"Congratulations!" shouted Noel.

"Congratulations!" shouted Wolf and all the
other Private Eyes.

"You have a good eye for clues," someone
said, "good enough to be a Private Eye."

"I can't believe it!" said Raoul. "You mean
you did all this?"

"Of course we did," said Wolf.

126

"We knew you wanted to be a Private Eye,"
Noel added. "So we gave you a mystery to solve."

"Wait a minute," Wolf cut in, noticing Sonia.
"What's she doing here?"

"Sonia's my partner," Raoul explained. "We
solved this mystery together."

"That's right," said Sonia. "Two pairs of
eyes turned out to be better than one."

"Listen, everybody," said Noel. "Since Sonia
had as much to do with solving the mystery as
Raoul, I vote we let her into our club too.
All those in favor say aye!"

"Aye!" came the loud reply.

"Then the ayes have it!" Noel shouted.

"And the Eyes have us!" said Raoul and Sonia
at exactly the same time. Then they looked at
one another and began to laugh happily.

Comprehension Check

1. At the beginning of the story, what did Raoul want more than anything else?
2. Why do you think the Private Eyes left the first note on Raoul's bicycle?
3. Where did Raoul find his second clue?
4. Do you think Raoul and Sonia did a good job of solving the mystery? Why or why not?
5. Pretend you are in the Private Eyes Club. What kind of mystery would you want a new member to solve?

Skill Check

Read the sentences below. Decide what happened in each sentence. Then decide why it happened.

1. Raoul thought the first note was a joke so he started to tear it up.
2. Raoul went to look for an oak tree because he wanted to find the next clue.
3. The children walked around Jake's truck to see if they could find the clue.
4. Sonia was made a member of the Private Eyes since she and Raoul solved the mystery together.

The Dance Theatre of Harlem

by Madeline Sunshine

It's theatre. It's music. It's colors and costumes and magical lights. But more than that, it's learning and constant practice. It's hard work and striving to be the best. It's the Dance Theatre of Harlem!

The Dance Theatre of Harlem is one of the newest ballet companies in the world. It was started in 1969 in Harlem. Harlem is a black community in New York City.

The Dance Theatre began as the dream of one man, Arthur Mitchell. Now the dream is more than just Arthur Mitchell's. It's shared by all the dancers, dance students, and audiences of the Dance Theatre of Harlem.

The Dance Theatre of Harlem has traveled all over the world. The company has danced in England, Europe, Mexico, and South America. And wherever they go, audiences find them exciting, creative, and beautiful to watch.

As a very young man, Arthur Mitchell studied dance at the School of American Ballet. He also studied with Karel Shook, a teacher and ballet master of the National Dance Theatre of Holland. Mr. Shook is now Arthur Mitchell's partner. He too works with the Dance Theatre of Harlem.

After only five years of study and practice, Mr. Mitchell's talents were recognized. He then became one of the star dancers of the New York City Ballet Company.

Dance Theatre of Harlem was started because of Arthur Mitchell's love of dance. It was also a way for him to work within the Harlem community. That's where Arthur Mitchell was born and raised. But more than anything else, Dance Theatre of Harlem was Arthur Mitchell's way of remembering Dr. Martin Luther King.

Dr. King was a black leader who died in 1968. He inspired many people, both black and white. Mr. Mitchell was one of these people. When Dr. King died, Arthur Mitchell wanted to do something special to show how much he cared. He says, "I asked myself, 'Arthur Mitchell, what can *you* do?' When you pay homage, you do the thing you do best: If you make music, you beat your drum; if you are a singer, you sing; if you are a dancer, you dance." So Arthur Mitchell danced. And so did the Dance Theatre of Harlem.

In the beginning, Dance Theatre of Harlem was very small. Mr. Mitchell found a place to work in the basement of a Harlem church. At that time there were only two professional dancers and thirty students. Mr. Mitchell wanted to attract more students. So he began what he calls the "open door" policy. This meant that anyone was allowed to drop in and take a class. Soon a number of girls and boys started coming to class regularly.

Within a short period of time, Mr. Mitchell realized the growing dance company needed more space. So he went looking for a larger, more permanent home for the company. At last he found the perfect place: an old garage in Harlem just two blocks from where he was born.

Arthur Mitchell has always tried to interest people in dance. He found many ways to do this. He gave dance demonstrations throughout the Harlem community. He also spoke about dance. He explained that learning to dance takes hard work and lots of training. He helped boys and girls to see that ballet is both an art and a form of physical exercise. He made his students understand that being a great dancer is the same thing as being a great athlete.

The company often gives performances for children. At each performance Mr. Mitchell invites some children from the audience to come up on stage. He asks them to do their favorite dance steps. Then he shows them how those same steps can be changed into ballet.

Many of Arthur Mitchell's beginning students were teenagers. Most ballet dancers begin studying at the age of eight. So these older students had a lot of catching up to do. Arthur Mitchell pushed and trained his students until they became the best dancers they could be.

To this day, Mr. Mitchell and his company welcome students of all ages to join in and dance. This policy has helped Dance Theatre of Harlem's school to grow and grow.

Arthur Mitchell always believed that ballet was more than just dancing to music. He felt it was like a musical play. Most of you have probably seen musicals in the movies, in theatres, or on television. For example, you may have seen *Peter Pan*, *Oklahoma*, or *The Wizard of Oz*, to name just a few. Arthur Mitchell wanted his ballets to include some of the wonderful things found in these kinds of musicals. He wanted to combine dance and acting, costumes and music. So he made sure his students learned all of these things.

Besides dance, some students were taught how to design and sew costumes for the company. Other students took singing lessons. Still other students studied rhythm instruments.

As well as being an excellent teacher and an incredible dancer, Mr. Mitchell is a fine choreographer. A choreographer is a person who composes the steps and sometimes the story of a ballet or dance.

Arthur Mitchell always draws from many sources in choreographing his ballets. Some of the ballets are based on African movements and rhythms. Others are more traditional ballets, such as *Swan Lake*. Dancers who work with the Dance Theatre of Harlem like the fact that Mr. Mitchell creates many different kinds of ballets for them to perform.

Besides performing for theatre audiences, the
company performs for the community. The group
gives shows once a month and invites
neighborhood people to come. They also perform
for children, senior citizens, and disabled people,
by inviting them to special performances at
nearby theatres. They bring a special kind of
joy to all the people for whom they perform.
Many people who had never been interested in
dance before began to enjoy it by watching
Arthur Mitchell and his company at work.

138

When Arthur Mitchell started the Dance
Theatre of Harlem, he wanted to show that a
black ballet company could achieve fame in the
dance world. He has accomplished this in a very
short period of time.

Now, wherever Arthur Mitchell and his company
travel, there's theatre and music, colors and
costumes, magical lights, and DANCE!

Comprehension Check

1. How did Arthur Mitchell try to interest people in studying at the Dance Theatre of Harlem school?
2. Why do you think Arthur Mitchell thinks that being a great dancer is the same as being a great athlete?
3. When Arthur Mitchell started the Dance Theatre of Harlem, he wanted to show that a black ballet company could achieve fame in the dance world. Do you think Mr. Mitchell was successful in achieving his goal? Why or why not?
4. Would you like to study ballet? Why or why not?

Skill Check

Answer the following questions about the details in the story you just read.

1. In what year was the Dance Theatre of Harlem started?
2. What was the first home of the Dance Theatre of Harlem?
3. Where is the home of the Dance Theatre of Harlem now?
4. What are the different things Arthur Mitchell combines when creating a ballet?
5. Besides dance, what are some of the other things taught at the Dance Theatre of Harlem school?
6. In what ways does the Dance Theatre of Harlem work within its community?

140

Adding Prefixes to Words

In the cartoon Joey says that he is afraid. Santo says that he is unafraid. Do these words mean the same thing? The words afraid and unafraid look very much alike, but the meanings of these words are very different.

The letters un- were added to the beginning of the word afraid to make the word unafraid. Un- is called a prefix. A **prefix** is added to the beginning of a word. When a prefix is added to a word, the new word has a different meaning.

The prefix un- means "not" or "do the opposite of." So the word unafraid means "not afraid."

In the next paragraph, Joey uses a word with the prefix un-. Do you know what the word means?

A little while later, the monster ate a roller coaster. "Hey!" cried Joey. "That was unfair! Leave the roller coaster alone!"

The prefix un- was added to the word fair to make the word unfair. The word unfair means "not fair."

In the first cartoon, Santo says that he hopes they reshow this part. The word reshow has a prefix added to it. The prefix is re-. The prefix re- means "again." When the prefix re- was added to the beginning of the word show, it changed the meaning of the word to "show again."

142

What does the word with the prefix re- mean
in the next paragraph?

Santo and Joey had been drinking milk
during the TV movie. The news came on,
and Santo went to the kitchen to refill
the glasses.

The prefix re- was added to the word fill to
make the word refill. Since the prefix re- means
"again," the word refill means "to fill again."
In the next paragraph is another word that
has the prefix re-. Do you know what it means?

"The Muncher is a silly name for a
movie," said Santo. "They should rename
it."

Did you look for the word that the prefix
was added to? It was added to the word name.
Did you remember that the prefix re- means
"again"? Then you probably figured out that the
word rename means "to name again."

Practice

What do the underlined words in these sentences mean?

1. Santo had baseball practice, so he was <u>unable</u> to watch the whole movie.
2. The monster was <u>unsure</u> if it wanted to eat the Golden Gate <u>Bridge</u>.
3. In the end, the monster decided to help <u>rebuild</u> the city.
4. <u>After</u> the movie, Joey decided to <u>reread</u> his homework.
5. Santo got home late from baseball practice, so his dinner had to be <u>reheated</u>.

As you read the story "Tall Tina," use the prefixes <u>un</u>- and <u>re</u>- to help you figure out the meanings of some of the words.

144

Tall Tina

by Muriel Stanek

When Tina was little, everybody at home called her Tiny Tina. But as she grew taller and taller and went to school, only her Grandma still called her Tiny Tina.

"My Tiny Tina is getting tall," she would say, "and that's just fine. There are lots of tall people in our family."

It was true. Most of Tina's family was tall. Tina liked that. She was proud to look like her family.

At school Tina was the tallest girl in her class. Most of the time that was fine with Tina. Her teacher would say, "Tina, please rearrange the papers on the top shelf in the closet."

"Not everyone can do that," Tina would tell herself happily.

Tina had long legs and she could run very
fast. On the way to school, she would call to
Robbie, "Bet you can't catch me!"

"You're right," Robbie would say. "You always
win because you have such long legs."

Sometimes, of course, Tina was unhappy about
being tall. At school she was tired of sitting
in the last seat in her row. And at home she
was getting too tall to squeeze down into her
favorite hiding place under the little round
table. Also, because Tina was so tall, everyone
expected her to act as grown-up as Beth. Beth
was Tina's older sister. But Tina wasn't as
grown-up as Beth, and that sometimes made things
hard.

146

One day a new boy named Jonathan moved into Tina's neighborhood. He was in her class at school. One afternoon, when they were on their way home, Jonathan shouted, "Tina is a string bean! String Bean Tina!"

A few of the children laughed. Then somebody else called out, "Tall Tina! Look at Tall Tina!"

Tina was so upset she ran home without looking back at anyone.

The next morning there was a note on Tina's desk. When she unfolded it, she read, "Tina is a" and there was a picture of a giraffe.

Tears filled Tina's eyes. "It's not my fault if I'm tall," she said to herself. Then she slid all the way down in her seat so she would look shorter.

That night Tina tried walking with her knees bent and her shoulders stooped.

"How come you're walking like that?" her sister Beth wanted to know.

"I have to look shorter," Tina answered.

"Why?" said Beth. "Mother and Aunt Mary are tall and they don't care."

But Tina *did* care. She couldn't help it. Lately nothing seemed like much fun to her. She began to think everyone was laughing at her because she was tall. She even started staying inside during school recess.

One afternoon when Tina was walking home, she saw Jonathan running behind her. She sure didn't want to see *him*. So she ran as fast as she could toward a big fence. She quickly hid behind it and peeked out from between its boards.

As Jonathan came closer, she saw that he was not running after her at all. As a matter of fact, two boys were chasing him!

All at once Jonathan tripped and fell. He hit his nose so hard it began to bleed. There was a big bump on his forehead too.

While Tina watched, the two boys ran up and laughed at Jonathan. He had his hand to his nose and tears were running down his cheeks.

"Crybaby!" yelled the boys as they ran off.

Tina stayed behind the fence until the two boys had gone. She was all set to say, "Ha, ha, Jonathan. Serves you right! Now you know how it feels to have someone make fun of you."

But when Tina finally walked over to Jonathan, she didn't yell at him at all. She couldn't. She felt too sorry for him.

Tina handed Jonathan a handkerchief. He wiped his nose and slowly got up. Tina helped him pick up his books and repack them in his book bag.

Tina and Jonathan walked down the street together without saying a word. At Jonathan's house, they stopped and looked at one another. Jonathan's nose had stopped bleeding, and the bump on his head didn't look too bad.

"Want to see my new kitten, Tina?" he asked.

Tina wondered if her ears were playing tricks on her. This was the first time Jonathan had ever used her right name. And what's more, he wasn't making fun of her.

"Maybe he isn't so bad after all," she thought. Still, she wasn't sure she really wanted to be friendly yet.

"My mother is waiting for me," she said. "I'll stop and see your kitten some other time."

As she walked on toward home, nobody called "Tall Tina!" or "String Bean!" That felt good.

The next morning Tina looked at her desk to see if there were any mean notes from Jonathan. There weren't any. When she went outside, she listened to hear if anyone called her a teasing name. No one did. Tina felt wonderful.

A few days later, on a warm day, the class was out in the playground. The gym teacher said, "We're going to have relay races. Jonathan will be the captain of one team. Dora will be the captain of the other team. Captains, choose your teams!"

Dora chose Mark for her team. Then it was Jonathan's turn to choose.

"I choose Tina!" he said, pointing at her.

"Why should I be on his team?" Tina asked herself. Still, she walked over to Jonathan.

The teams lined up. The shortest runners were first and the tallest last. Mark was last on Dora's team. Tina was last on Jonathan's.

"On your mark. Get set. Go!" called the gym teacher.

Dora and Jonathan raced to the fence and then back to the next runners in line. The teams were so evenly matched it was hard to tell which would win.

As they waited their turn, Tina and Mark jumped up and down with excitement. Tina felt she had to win. Mark felt the very same way.

It was a close race right to the very end.

"Run, Tina, run!" yelled Jonathan. Tina ran as hard as she could. She had to beat Mark, she just had to. Tina's long legs carried her over the finish line slightly ahead of him. She had done it! She had won for her team!

Everybody cheered. Jonathan shouted, "We won!" the loudest of all, and he gave Tina a big smile.

That night, when Tina looked in the mirror, she stood straight and tall. She didn't stoop or slump. Being tall was a pretty good thing, she decided. She felt glad to be her tall self and to be part of a tall family.

Comprehension Check

1. What did Jonathan do to upset Tina?
2. Why did Tina start staying inside during school recess?
3. Why do you think Jonathan stopped making fun of Tina?
4. Have you ever been in a relay race? What other kinds of races have you been in?

Skill Check

Tell what the underlined words mean in the following sentences.

1. "Tina, please rearrange the papers on the top shelf in the closet."
2. Sometimes, of course, Tina was unhappy about being tall.
3. When Tina unfolded the note, she read, "Tina is a" and there was a picture of a giraffe.
4. Tina helped him pick up his books and repack them in his book bag.

by A. A. Milne

Edward Bear, known to his friends as Winnie-
the-Pooh, or Pooh for short, was walking through
the forest one day, humming proudly to himself.
He had made up a little hum that very morning,
as he was doing his Stoutness Exercises in
front of the glass.

Tra-la-la, tra-la-la, as he stretched up as
high as he could go, and then *Tra-la-la, tra-
la-oh, help!-la,* as he tried to reach his toes.

After breakfast he had said it over and over
to himself until he had learned it by heart,
and now he was humming it right through,
properly. It went like this:

Literary Unit

Tra-la-la, tra-la-la,
Tra-la-la, tra-la,la,
Rum-tum-tiddle-um-tum.
Tiddle-iddle, tiddle-iddle,
Tiddle-iddle, tiddle-iddle,
Rum-tum-tum-tiddle-um.

Well, he was humming this hum to himself, and walking along gaily, wondering what everybody else was doing, and what it felt like being somebody else, when suddenly he came to a sandy bank, and in the bank was a large hole.

"Aha!" said Pooh. "*Rum-tum-tiddle-um-tum.* If I know anything about anything, that hole means Rabbit," he said, "and Rabbit means Company," he said, "and Company means Food and Listening-to-Me-Humming and such like. *Rum-tum-tum-tiddle-um.*"

So he bent down, put his head into the hole, and called out, "Is anybody at home?"

There was a sudden scuffling noise from inside the hole, and then silence.

"What I said was, 'Is anybody at home?'" called out Pooh very loudly.

"No!" said a voice, and then added, "You needn't shout so loud. I heard you quite well the first time."

"Bother!" said Pooh. "Isn't there anybody here at all?"

"Nobody."

Winnie-the-Pooh took his head out of the hole and thought for a little, and he thought to himself, "There must be somebody there, because somebody must have said, 'Nobody.'" So he put his head back in the hole and said, "Hallo, Rabbit, isn't that you?"

"No," said Rabbit, in a different sort of voice this time.

"But isn't that Rabbit's voice?"

"I don't think so," said Rabbit. "It isn't meant to be."

"Oh!" said Pooh.

He took his head out of the hole and had another think, and then he put it back and said, "Well, could you very kindly tell me where Rabbit is?"

"He has gone to see his friend Pooh Bear, who is a great friend of his."

"But this *is* Me!" said Bear, very much surprised.

"What sort of Me?"

"Pooh Bear."

"Are you sure?" said Rabbit, still more surprised.

"Quite, quite sure," said Pooh.

"Oh, well, then, come in."

So Pooh pushed and pushed and pushed his way through the hole, and at last he got in.

"You were quite right," said Rabbit, looking at him all over. "It *is* you. Glad to see you."

"Who did you think it was?"

"Well, I wasn't sure. You know how it is in the Forest. One can't have *anybody* coming into one's house. One has to be *careful*. What about a mouthful of something?"

Pooh always liked a little something at eleven o'clock in the morning, and he was very glad to see Rabbit getting out the plates and mugs; and when Rabbit said, "Honey or condensed milk with your bread?" he was so excited that he said, "Both," and then, so as not to seem greedy, he added, "But don't bother about the bread, please." And for a long time after that he said nothing . . . until at last, humming to himself in a rather sticky voice, he got up, shook Rabbit lovingly by the paw, and said that he must be going on.

"Must you?" said Rabbit politely.

"Well," said Pooh, "I could stay a little longer if it—if you—" and he tried very hard not to look in the direction of the larder.

"As a matter of fact," said Rabbit, "I was going out myself directly."

"Oh, well, then, I'll be going on. Good-by."

"Well, good-by, if you're sure you won't have any more."

"*Is* there any more?" asked Pooh quickly.

Rabbit took the covers off the dishes and said, "No, there wasn't."

"I thought not," said Pooh, nodding to himself. "Well, good-by. I must be going on."

So he started to climb out of the hole. He pulled with his front paws and pushed with his back paws, and in a little while his nose was out in the open again . . . and then his ears . . . and then his front paws . . . and then his shoulders . . . and then—

"Oh, help!" said Pooh. "I'd better go back."

"Oh, bother!" said Pooh. "I shall have to go on."

"I can't do either!" said Pooh. "Oh, help *and* bother!"

Now by this time Rabbit wanted to go for a walk too, and finding the front door full, he went out by the back door, and came round to Pooh, and looked at him.

"Hallo, are you stuck?" he asked.

"N-no," said Pooh carelessly. "Just resting and thinking and humming to myself."

Literary Unit

"Here, give us a paw."

Pooh Bear stretched out a paw, and Rabbit pulled and pulled and pulled. . . .

"*Ow!*" cried Pooh. "You're hurting!"

"The fact is," said Rabbit, "you're stuck."

"It all comes," said Pooh crossly, "of not having front doors big enough."

"It all comes," said Rabbit sternly, "of eating too much. I thought at the time," said Rabbit, "only I didn't like to say anything," said Rabbit, "that one of us was eating too much," said Rabbit, "and I knew it wasn't *me,*" he said. "Well, well, I shall go and fetch Christopher Robin."

Christopher Robin lived at the other end of the Forest, and when he came back with Rabbit and saw the front half of Pooh, he said, "Silly old Bear," in such a loving voice that everybody felt quite hopeful again.

"I was just beginning to think," said Bear, sniffing slightly, "that Rabbit might never be able to use his front door again. And I should *hate* that," he said.

"So should I," said Rabbit.

"Use his front door again?" said Christopher Robin. "Of course he'll use his front door again."

"Good," said Rabbit.

"If we can't pull you out, Pooh, we might push you back."

Rabbit scratched his whiskers thoughtfully and pointed out that, when Pooh was pushed back, he was back, and of course nobody was more glad to see Pooh than *he* was, still there it was, some lived in trees and some lived underground and—

"You mean I'd *never* get out?" said Pooh.

"I mean," said Rabbit, "that having got *so* far, it seems a pity to waste it."

Christopher Robin nodded. "Then there's only one thing to be done," he said. "We shall have to wait for you to get thin again."

"How long does getting thin take?" asked Pooh anxiously.

"About a week, I should think."

"But I can't stay here for a *week!*"

"You can *stay* here all right, silly old Bear. It's getting you out which is so difficult."

"We'll read to you," said Rabbit cheerfully. "And I hope it won't snow," he added. "And I say, old fellow, you're taking up a good deal of room in my house—*do* you mind if I use your back legs as a towel-horse? Because, I mean, there they are—doing nothing—and it would be very convenient just to hang the towels on them."

"A week!" said Pooh gloomily. *"What about meals?"*

"I'm afraid no meals," said Christopher Robin, "because of getting thin quicker. But we *will* read to you."

Bear began to sigh, and then found he couldn't because he was so tightly stuck; and a tear rolled down his eye as he said, "Then would you read a Sustaining Book, such as would help and comfort a Wedged Bear in Great Tightness?"

So for a week Christopher Robin read that sort of book at the North end of Pooh, and Rabbit hung his washing on the South end . . . and in between Bear felt himself getting slenderer and slenderer.

And at the end of the week Christopher Robin said, *"Now!"* So he took hold of Pooh's front paws, and Rabbit took hold of Christopher Robin, and all Rabbit's friends and relations took hold of Rabbit, and they all pulled together. . . .

And for a long time Pooh only said, *"Ow!"* . . . And *"Oh!"*

And then, all of a sudden, he said, *"Pop!"* just as if a cork were coming out of a bottle.

And Christopher Robin and Rabbit and all Rabbit's friends and relations went head-over-heels backwards . . . and on top of them came Winnie-the-Pooh—free!

So, with a nod of thanks to his friends, he went on with his walk through the Forest, humming proudly to himself. But Christopher Robin looked after him lovingly, and said to himself, "Silly old Bear!"

SECTION TWO

Mary of Mile 18

by Ann Blades

It is a cold winter in northern British Columbia. At the Fehr farm snow has covered the ground since early November, and it will not melt until May.

One clear night in February the temperature drops to forty degrees below zero and the northern lights flash across the sky. Mary Fehr gets out of bed and goes to the window to watch and listen. She hears a crackling sound and smiles, excited. Mary likes to pretend that if she hears the music of the lights, the next day will bring something special.

170

The next morning Mary Fehr wakes up happy. At first she can't think why. Then she remembers, and wonders what the day will bring.
She pulls on her boots, hat, heavy coat, and mittens, and walks to the hen house to feed the chickens.

Mary sees her father near the barn. The tractor was damaged yesterday, and he is trying to fix it. Every winter day when it does not snow, Mr. Fehr likes to clear a little more land. He uses the tractor to push the trees down and into piles.

When summer comes all the family will pick roots, tearing them out of the earth with their hands so that the land can be planted.

Before he comes in for breakfast, Mr. Fehr puts a propane torch under the truck to warm the engine. It will take an hour to warm because last night was so cold.

After breakfast Mr. Fehr goes out first and starts the engine. He lets it run for a while, then honks the horn. Mary, her sister, Sarah, and her brothers, Jake and Isaac, come out and crowd into the seat beside him.

Today the teacher, Mrs. Burns, has turned the oil heater on full, but the room is still so cold that the children sitting beside the windows keep their coats on and edge closer to the heater.

At three o'clock it is time to go home. Mary helps dress the smaller children. She sighs as she pulls on her own overshoes. School is over and still nothing special has happened.

In the truck on the way home, Mr. Fehr listens to the children talk about school but does not talk himself. He is watching the road carefully. Snow is drifting and it is hard to see.

Just as they near the farm, another truck looms out of the blowing snow. Mr. Fehr steers quickly to the right to avoid an accident and his back wheels slide into the ditch.

As Mary watches her father jack up the truck and put chains on the rear tires, she thinks, "I hope that's not the special thing."

Then, farther up the road to the house, Mary sees something in the snow and cries, "Look, a puppy." She runs to him, kneels down, and the puppy licks her mitten.

The pup snuggles in Mary's arms. How she wishes she could keep him! "I would call you Wolf," she says.

Mary carries the pup to the truck. "Please, Father, can I keep him?"

Mr. Fehr shakes his head. "You know the rules. Our animals must work for us or give us food."

Mary protests: "A dog can help . . ."

Mr. Fehr interrupts: "That isn't a regular dog. He's part wolf, and wolf pups are useless. Take him into the woods and leave him. He'll be all right. Come on, the rest of you. Chores."

Sadly Mary goes off with the pup while the other children go about their chores. When she returns to the house, it smells of fresh-baked bread. Her mother meets her at the door.

"Where have you been, Mary? Sarah is waiting for you. I'm almost out of water."

Silently Mary bends down, takes two empty buckets standing near the door, and goes out.

Sarah has already filled her buckets with snow. Mary does the same, and the two girls carry the snow into the house and dump it into a big barrel. They wait for it to melt, then go out for more snow.

Each time Mary goes out, she looks toward the woods. Her father comes out of the barn where he has been feeding the pigs and goes into the house. The pup is nowhere in sight.

The coal lamp is lit. Mary sits at the table staring at her reader. The radio says another cold night, and Mary thinks about the pup.

Suddenly there is a sound outside the door, a low whimper. Mr. Fehr goes to the door and opens it. Mary cries, "It's little Wolf," and rushes to take the pup in her arms.

Mr. Fehr is angry. "Mary, you shouldn't encourage him to stay around. Take him out again and don't let him follow you back."

This time Mary walks nearly two miles to the Bergen farm, their closest neighbor. "Perhaps Mr. Bergen will let his children keep you," she says, putting Wolf down near the door. "Then I can see you sometimes."

As she runs home in the cold night her toes and fingertips sting and the air burns her throat.

The family is at the supper table when she gets back. "We have your favorite supper tonight, Mary. Moose steak," said her mother.

"I don't want to eat, Mother."

Mrs. Fehr starts to object, but Mr. Fehr stops her: "Let Mary go to bed without eating if she wants to." His voice is still angry. "She should not have asked to keep the animal. She knows the rules."

Mary gets into bed and buries her head in her pillow. "Why should he be so angry?" she wonders. Then she remembers her mother saying once: "Your father gives you everything he can. When you ask for more, it hurts him to refuse. That is why he gets angry."

Mary lies thinking about this until she falls asleep.

Literary Unit

That night when everyone in the Fehr house is asleep, another kind of animal, a coyote, comes out of the woods. He sniffs at all the buildings, then stops at the hen house. Silently he paws at the rope that holds the door shut, and the rope comes loose. The coyote pushes the door to enter the hen house.

Suddenly, a shrill screech goes up in the night. Everyone in the Fehr house wakes up. Mr. Fehr throws his clothes on quickly, grabs his gun, and goes out.

The rest of the family get up and crowd around the window to see what is happening. All except Mary. She tries to go back to sleep, so that she won't have to think about little Wolf out in the woods.

Mr. Fehr sees the coyote in the bright light from the snow. He aims his gun and fires. His first shot misses. The coyote turns, snarling, then quickly runs behind the hen house. Mr. Fehr fires again, but the coyote takes off and disappears over the hill.

Mr. Fehr goes to the hen house, looks inside to make sure the chickens are all right. Then he carefully ties the door tight. He is about to return to the house when he sees something at his feet. It is the wolf pup wagging his tail.

"So it was you who warned us," Mr. Fehr says. He bends down, takes the puppy in his hands, and looks at him. "Tough little fellow, aren't you? Not afraid of cold or coyotes. Maybe you will earn your keep after all."

He carries the pup into the house. Mrs. Fehr has lit the oil lamp, and everyone is waiting for him, except Mary.

The children are excited when they see the wolf pup. Mr. Fehr puts his finger to his lips as a sign for them to be silent. He goes to the bedroom.

Mary looks up as her father comes into the bedroom. He puts the wolf pup down on the bed. "This little fellow would like to get warm," he says.

Mary can hardly believe she is not dreaming as she takes little Wolf in her arms. "Can I keep him?" she asks.

"I suppose you can," her father answers gruffly.

In the doorway of the bedroom, Isaac and Jake and Sarah and Mrs. Fehr are all standing, watching and smiling.

Comprehension Check

1. What did Mary find in the snow?
2. Why didn't Mary want to eat her supper?
3. Why do you think Mr. Fehr changed his mind about keeping the pup?
4. Would you like to live in a farmhouse in the country? Why or why not?

180

My Puppy

by Aileen Fisher

It's funny
my puppy
knows just how I feel.

When I'm happy
he's yappy
and squirms like an eel.

When I'm grumpy
he's slumpy
and stays at my heel.

It's funny
my puppy
knows such a great deal.

The Three Wonderful Seeds

by Gloria Logan

Once upon a time an old woman, walking in the woods, found some strange-looking seeds. "I will take these three seeds home and plant them," she said. "And we shall see what we shall see."

So the old woman took the three seeds home and planted them in the warm earth by the kitchen door. Every morning she got up and looked to see if the three seeds had come up.

"I have planted three seeds," said she. "But I do not know what will come up."

182

One morning the old woman found her little red rooster scratching around in the garden. Before she could stop him, the little rooster had eaten one of the strange seeds.

"Now there are only two seeds to come up," sighed the old woman. "But we shall see. Yes, we shall see."

The next day it rained and rained. When the old woman went to see if the seeds had come up yet, she could only find one. The other seed had been washed away by the rain.

"Now there is only one seed to come up," sighed the old woman. "But we shall see. Yes, we shall see."

And she built a little fence around the seed.

The last little seed lay sleeping for a long time. The sun warmed the earth around it. The soft rain pattered down and whispered that it was time the little seed was waking up. So one day the little seed cracked open and put out two pretty green leaves.

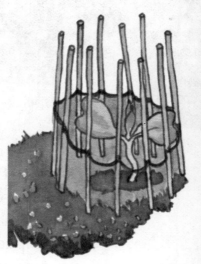

The old woman looked after the little plant carefully, and it grew bigger each day. "I have a most wonderful plant," said the old woman. "But I do not know what it is."

By and by the people came to see the old woman's wonderful plant.

"It is a magic plant," said one.

"It is a weed," said another.

"It is a Present Plant," said a child.

"Perhaps it is," said the old woman. "We shall see."

All summer long the plant grew. People came to see the buds open. Everyone wondered what sort of flowers the wonderful plant would have when the buds opened.

Very soon they found out. One morning the old woman found that the buds had opened in the night and the little plant's branches were loaded with strangely shaped boxes and bundles.

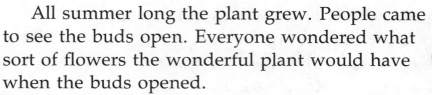

"Oh, my goodness," said the old woman. "It is just what the child said it was. It is a Present Plant. Now isn't that something!"

The old woman put out her hand and took one of the packages. Inside the bundle she found a warm red scarf. "Just what I wanted," she said happily. "Now I shall tell everyone to come and pick a present from the plant."

184

"It certainly is a wonderful thing, this Present Plant," said all the people.

More buds came on the plant. It seemed that as soon as someone picked off a present, another grew in its place. The children loved the plant, and no one picked more than one present.

By and by the king's daughter heard of the wonderful Present Plant. She came to see it growing in the old woman's garden.

The princess picked the biggest package on the plant. When she opened it, there was a beautiful china horse. The horse was a lovely shade of golden yellow. Its mane and tail were snowy white.

"Humph," the princess grumbled. "It is not very pretty. I shall just pick another one."

"Oh, Princess," whispered the old woman. "No one ever takes more than one present."

"I am a princess," said the princess. "I shall take as many as I like. Isn't that right, Father?"

The king nodded. "Of course, my dear. Help yourself. They say the presents grow right back on again, so there's no harm."

So the princess picked and picked. Even when she had her arms full of packages and was too busy to open them, she kept right on picking the bundles that bloomed on the old woman's Present Plant.

"See, old woman," she said. "Nothing has happened. The presents are still growing."

"Wait and see," said the old woman. "It is not right to be so greedy, even if you are a princess."

When the princess was in the royal carriage, she began to open her gifts. But a strange thing happened. All the wonderful presents were gone. Instead, there were only a few limp blossoms and brown petals. And in a little while these too curled up and drifted away in the wind.

Only the beautiful china horse, the first present the princess had chosen, remained. She held the horse carefully and was very quiet all the way to the palace.

As for the wonderful plant that grew in the old woman's garden, it is still there. But no one, not even a princess, may pick more than one present. When they do, they find nothing in their hands but a limp white blossom that soon drifts away.

188

Comprehension Check

1. What did the old woman do to protect the last seed from being eaten or washed away?
2. What present did the old woman pick off the Present Plant?
3. Do you think the princess was used to having her own way? Why or why not?
4. How do you think the old woman felt when she saw the princess picking so many presents?
5. If you could pick a present off a Present Plant, what would you like to find inside?

Skill Check

How many vowel sounds are there in each word below? How many syllables are there?

1. nodded
2. garden
3. old
4. three
5. princess
6. right

How would you divide the following words into two syllables?

1. summer
2. nothing
3. blossoms
4. yellow
5. package
6. wonder

Skill Lesson

Using a Dictionary or Glossary for Pronunciation

A dictionary and glossary show you how to pronounce entry words. Look at this entry for the word cruise.

Symbols

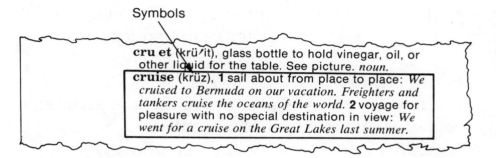

cru et (krü′it), glass bottle to hold vinegar, oil, or other liquid for the table. See picture. *noun.*

cruise (krüz), **1** sail about from place to place: *We cruised to Bermuda on our vacation. Freighters and tankers cruise the oceans of the world.* **2** voyage for pleasure with no special destination in view: *We went for a cruise on the Great Lakes last summer.*

The letters and marks in parentheses that follow the entry word are **symbols.** These symbols stand for sounds. The symbols show you how to pronounce the word.

A **pronunciation key** tells you what the symbols stand for. It is usually found in the front of a dictionary or glossary. The pronunciation key for the glossary in this book can be found on page 335.

Look at the pronunciation key on page 335. There is a key word next to each symbol. The sound each symbol stands for is the same as the sound you hear in the key word.

Find the u in the pronunciation key. This is the sound you hear in the u in cup and

190

butter. Now find the ü. This is the sound you hear in the u in rule and the o in move.

To pronounce a word, match the symbols in the entry with the symbols in the key.

How is the word cruise pronounced? Use the symbols in the pronunciation key to help you. The word cruise rhymes with the word lose. Are you surprised?

Here is the entry for the word ballast.

Accent Mark

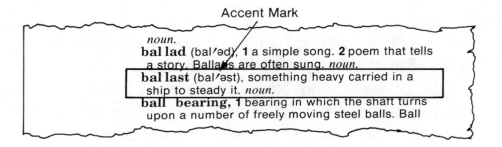

noun.
bal lad (bal′əd), **1** a simple song. **2** poem that tells a story. Ballads are often sung. *noun.*
bal last (bal′əst), something heavy carried in a ship to steady it. *noun.*
ball bearing, 1 bearing in which the shaft turns upon a number of freely moving steel balls. Ball

Ballast is printed in two syllables. Look at the symbols in the entry. They tell you what each syllable sounds like. Do you see the heavy black mark between the syllables? It is called an **accent mark.** The accent mark tells you which syllable should be said more strongly.

Say the word ballast. Which syllable is stronger? Yes, the first syllable of ballast is stronger. That is why the accent mark comes right after the first syllable.

Look at the second syllable in the word ballast. Do you see the little upside-down e? This symbol (ə) is called a **schwa.** The schwa sound is a vowel sound. It is heard only in

syllables that are not accented. Look at the sample words for the schwa sound shown below.

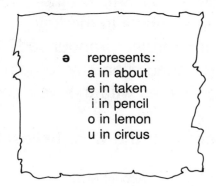

ə   represents:
a in about
e in taken
i in pencil
o in lemon
u in circus

The schwa sound can be spelled many different ways. Say the sample words to yourself. Listen for the schwa sound. Now say the word ballast. Do you hear the schwa sound? The schwa sound is heard in the second syllable. It is not the syllable that is accented.

Practice

Look below at the entry for the word canoe. Use the pronunciation key on page 335 and the entry to answer the questions that follow.

can non ball (kan′ən bol′), a large, solid iron or steel ball, that used to be fired from cannons. *noun.*

can not (kan′ot *or* ka not′), can not. *verb.*

ca noe (kə nü′), **1** a light boat pointed at both ends and moved with a paddle. See picture. **2** paddle a canoe; go in a canoe. 1 *noun,* 2 *verb,* **ca noed, ca noe ing.**

can o py (kan′ə pē), a covering fixed over a bed, throne, or entrance, or carried on poles over a person. See picture. *noun, plural* **can o pies.**

can't (kant), can not.

1. Is the accent mark on the first or second syllable?
2. The symbol k stands for the sound you hear in what words in the pronunciation key?
3. The schwa ə stands for the sound you hear in what words in the pronunciation key?
4. The symbol ü stands for the sound you hear in what words in the pronunciation key?

If you come across any words you can't pronounce in the selection "Wild Canada Geese," use a dictionary or the glossary at the back of this book to help you pronounce them.

Wild Canada Geese

by Nadra Holmes

What makes a musical sound like a trumpet, but can't be found in any orchestra? It's a beautiful bird called the Canada goose.

The Canada goose is the most famous of all wild geese. It has a light-colored "chinstrap" of feathers around its throat. Its body and wings are a brownish color, and its long neck and head are black. This long neck works like a trumpet. It gives the Canada goose its rich, musical, honking voice.

Canada geese do not live in one place. They migrate, or travel, thousands of miles each year. They migrate in flocks. A flock can be made up of as many as one hundred birds.

194

How fast do you think Canada geese fly? Many years ago a man by the name of Jack Miner wanted to find out the answer to this question. So, when a flock of Canada geese came down to rest at his bird sanctuary in Ontario, Canada, he decided to study them. While they rested at the sanctuary, he watched them very closely. Then, as soon as they took off, he telegraphed to friends who lived up ahead.

The next morning large flocks of geese were seen flying over a town 490 miles (about 784 kilometers) north of Jack Miner's sanctuary. If these were the same geese, their flying speed would have been thirty-five to forty miles per hour. Scientists now believe that this is the average speed at which geese fly.

Today there are new and better ways of studying Canada geese.

Sometimes geese are caught and special bands are placed around their feet. This is called bird banding. On the band is a number and a date. After it is banded, the goose is set free.

If the goose is found by a scientist or is shot by a hunter, he or she will see the band. People who find these bands are asked to send them back to the government wildlife service. Every year thousands of bands are returned to the wildlife service. There, scientists keep careful records of where the bands were put on the geese and where they were later removed. They use these records to make maps of migration routes.

Bird banding does not hurt the goose. What it does is help scientists learn more about how and where the Canada goose travels.

Canada geese do not like to fly in bad
weather. Strong winds can blow them off course.
Fog can cause them to lose all sense of
direction.

In 1925 a large flock of Canada geese was
flying over a small town in Ohio when they ran
into a heavy fog. The birds had to come down.
Thousands of geese landed in city streets and
on the tops of houses. The people who lived in
the town were surprised. Some geese were shot
by hunters, but many escaped when the fog
lifted.

When Canada geese travel, they fly in a "V" formation. This means that one or two geese lead the flock and the rest follow, like the sides of the letter V. The leaders of the flock are always older geese. They follow a flight course from memory, returning to places where they were raised. Where and when they travel depends upon climate. Canada geese like to stay warm all year round.

During the summer Canada geese live in the northern United States and Canada. In early fall, when the air begins to turn cold, the geese fly south to Mexico and the Gulf states. Then when spring comes they go north again.

198

The Canada goose considers the North its home. It's there, in springtime, that the female goose builds a nest and prepares to lay eggs. The female goose builds and prepares her nest of roots, twigs, and grasses. Then she lines it with a few of her own soft down feathers.

The place she picks to build her nest is very important. It must be safe from animals who like to eat goose eggs. It must also be close to water and feeding grounds. Canada geese often nest on small islands or on the banks of lakes and rivers.

When the mother goose has made her nest, she lays one egg a day until she has six or seven creamy white eggs. She will leave the nest only a few times a day, to eat, drink, rest, and bathe. This allows the eggs to cool off. It is not good for goose eggs to stay too warm.

The male goose, or gander, stays close to the nest too. He and his mate are rarely separated.

It takes one month for the goose eggs to hatch. The baby, called a gosling, must break the shell with its beak and struggle out through the small opening it makes. This is very hard work. It takes almost a whole day. When the goslings finally do get out of their shells, they are wet, tired, and ready for sleep.

Goslings stay in their nests during the first night. They are soon able to walk, however, and the next morning they follow their parents to find food and water.

The parents teach their young how to eat marsh and water plants. When they hunt for food under water, Canada geese appear to be standing on their heads. This can be a very funny sight.

The parents also teach the goslings how to avoid snapping turtles and other enemies. But they do not have to teach them how to swim. As soon as they reach water, goslings are expert swimmers.

Canada geese have very strong family bonds. The goslings stay with their parents until they are about two years old. Then the young geese join other flocks and set out on their own.

Canada geese, like most birds and animals, have natural enemies. Natural enemies are usually other birds and animals that live in the same environment and compete for food. But the most dangerous enemy of the Canada goose is neither other birds nor other animals. This bird's most dangerous enemy is people.

Angry farmers who don't want the geese to feed on their wheat and rice crops often shoot the birds down. Hunters shoot at the birds for sport.

Because Canada geese cannot protect themselves from all their enemies, there are people who are trying to help them. These people are called conservationists. Conservationists try to help the birds live in safety. Every year the United States Fish and Wildlife Service checks the Canada goose population. Laws are passed to protect the geese from being hunted and killed.

Also, in Canada and the United States, special sanctuaries have been set up for geese. The sanctuaries give the birds a place to rest and feed safely. Hopefully, these sanctuaries will help the Canada goose to live on and on.

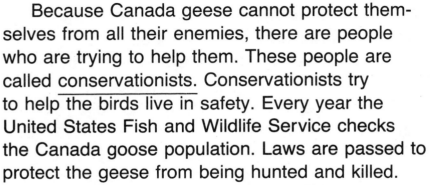

Comprehension Check

1. What does the Canada goose look like?
2. How long does it take for a Canada goose egg to hatch?
3. What does the female goose use to build her nest?
4. Why don't Canada geese like to fly in bad weather?
5. Do you think bird sanctuaries are a good way to protect Canada geese? Why or why not?
6. Are there other animals or birds that you would like to learn more about? Which ones?

Skill Check

Find the word migration in your glossary. Use the entry and the pronunciation key on page 335 to answer the questions that follow.

1. Is the accent mark on the first, second, or third syllable?
2. What vowel sound do you hear in the third syllable?
3. The symbol sh stands for the sound you hear in what word in the pronunciation key?
4. The schwa (ə) stands for the sound you hear in what words in the pronunciation key?

Peter's Brownstone House

by Hila Colman

Once, a long time ago, a beautiful house was built in New York City. It had a wide stoop and an iron railing with a gate in front.

Inside, the rooms were large, with high ceilings, and almost every room had a fireplace. Many of them had glittering chandeliers that were lighted with hundreds of tiny candles.

The stairway, with its banisters of smooth mahogany, was wide and graceful.

The people who built the house wanted it to last for many, many years. The house did last for many years, although it was slowly surrounded by tall buildings.

Even then people still lived in it: a boy
named Peter and his great-grandfather, whom he
called Grandpa.

Peter, however, hated the old house. He
wanted to live in the tall, new apartment
building across the way, where his best friend,
John, lived. Then he could ride up and down in
the elevator, and he could say good morning to
the jolly doorman.

But Grandpa loved his old, old house, and he
hated new apartment buildings. "Nothing is the
way it used to be," he grumbled.

One day a man came to see Grandpa. He wanted
to buy the old-fashioned brownstone, and he
offered a large sum of money for it.

"We want to tear it down," he said, "and put
up a modern apartment house."

206   *Skills Unit 12*

"Can we live in the new house when it is built?" Peter asked eagerly.

"Of course," the man said.

Peter was very excited, but Grandpa said he had to think it over. Peter wished he could get Grandpa to sell the old-fashioned house. "Why do you like this old house so much?" he asked him.

"I love it because it is old," Grandpa told him. "I was born in this house, and I used to play in the same playroom that you play in now. I don't like the idea of it being torn down. But I will think about it," he promised.

Grandpa thought and thought, but he could not make up his mind. "Let's go for a walk," he said to Peter. "Then I will think some more."

They walked up the street and down the avenue. Everywhere they looked old houses were being torn down and new houses were going up.

"The city is not the way it used to be when I was a boy," Grandpa said with a sigh. "Come on, I'll show you where *my* grandfather's house used to be."

Grandpa took Peter to a street between the park and the river. It was busy and noisy, and lots of children were playing on the sidewalk.

"See that drugstore on the corner?" Grandpa said. "My grandfather's farmhouse used to be there. And where those children are roller-skating is where I used to plant the corn."

They started to cross the street, and the police officer blew his whistle.

"Watch the lights," he called to them.

Grandpa took Peter by the hand. "My mind was way back in the past, when it was quiet and peaceful here. You could hear the birds singing and the cows mooing."

Now they were facing the river. "Let's go down to see the boats," Peter suggested. But they couldn't get near the river. Instead they saw huge buildings that Grandpa called docks behind high wire fences. Peter looked through the fence and watched a big crane lift an automobile from the deck of a freighter and lower it onto the dock.

"I wish I could go down to the water," Peter said.

"You could when I was a boy," Grandpa told him. "We used to go fishing down there. We fished right off the dock, and watched the sailboats come in. Sometimes a captain gave us a souvenir from India or Africa. Those sailboats were pretty in the harbor."

By now it was getting late, and all at once the street lights came on.

"It was very different in my day," Grandpa said. "The gaslighter went from lamp to lamp, lighting each lamp, one at a time. We didn't have electricity then."

When they got home, Peter sat in his favorite window seat and looked longingly at the apartment house across the way. Lights were twinkling in every window. But suddenly all the lights in the apartment house, the lights on the street, and the lights in his own house went out!

Grandpa called to him, "Peter, where are you? What happened?"

"I don't know," Peter called back.

210

Quickly he turned on his battery-operated radio. "There is a power failure in the city," the announcer said. "Most apartments in the area will have no heat, no lights, and no elevator service."

"Well, we'll be all right," Grandpa said with a chuckle. "You find some candles, and I'll build fires in the fireplaces."

Peter and Grandpa were very busy. Peter took a flashlight and found the candles. Grandpa brought in wood and made fires in the fire-places. Soon the fires were blazing. Grandpa lit the candles and put them on the mantel.

Peter looked around the living room. He thought he had never seen anything so beautiful. The candlelight and the firelight gave the room a soft, cozy glow and made the old wood and the chandelier shine.

Then Peter thought of his friend John in the apartment house.

"Grandpa," he cried. "I want to see if John is all right. Maybe he can't get home if the elevators aren't working."

"Let's go ask the doorman," Grandpa said.

They went across the street and found John in the lobby with the doorman. He was trying to get up the courage to walk up sixteen flights of stairs.

"It's a long climb," the doorman said.

"I know it," John agreed. "And when I get home it will be cold and dark."

"Come over to our house," Grandpa said. "We have lights and heat and we don't need an elevator. We can call your parents from there and tell them where you are."

"Hurray!" John cried, and they went back across the street together.

John and Peter had never known before what fun an old house could be. They added logs to the fire, and they ran up the stairs to Peter's room. They talked to each other on the old-fashioned house phones from one floor to the next. When it was time to eat, Grandpa cooked dinner on the old coal stove in the kitchen.

"I wish the electricity would never get fixed," John said. But just then the lights came on, and soon John had to go home. After he left, Peter was so happy he went to the top of the stairs and slid down the banister.

"This is better than an elevator," he cried.

The next day the man came back to ask Grandpa
if he had decided to sell the house.

"I'll ask my grandson," he told the man.
"Peter," Grandpa called to him, "come here and
tell the man if you want to sell this house."

"Oh, no!" Peter cried. "I wouldn't sell this
house for a million dollars. There are hundreds
of apartment houses, but there's only one house
like this in the whole city."

The man went away very disappointed.

Peter and Grandpa still live in their old
brownstone house. Whenever Peter passes the
apartment house across the way, he waves hello
to the jolly doorman. But he is glad that he
lives in his big, old-fashioned brownstone.

Skills Unit 12

Comprehension Check

1. At the beginning of the story, why did Peter want to move to a modern apartment building?
2. Why did a man come to see Grandpa?
3. Why did Peter turn on his battery-operated radio?
4. Why do you think Peter changed his mind about the old house?
5. If there was a power failure in your city or town, what could you do at home to make things more comfortable?

Skill Check

The underlined words in the sentences below are taken from the story you just read. In each sentence, find the word that has the same vowel sound as the underlined word.

1. The toy drum made a lot of noise.
2. The boy soiled his shirt.
3. Martha left food on the stoop for the cat.
4. Look at what Grandpa cooked for breakfast.
5. The town was famous for its prize-winning cows.
6. Jim watched the show from the third row.
7. The child climbed out of her crib.
8. Janet has to walk up six flights of stairs every night.
9. Bill rode to school on Marsha's old bicycle.

Chameleon Was a Spy

by Diane Redfield Massie

Chameleon liked to change colors. He could match the rug and the chair. "I can match anything," said Chameleon. "You name it!" Because of this special talent, Chameleon knew he could be a spy.

His big break came when he was hired by The Pleasant Pickle Company. Their formula for the world's best pickles had been stolen from them by the Perfect Pickle Company. That's where Chameleon is headed when the story begins.

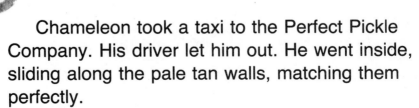

Chameleon took a taxi to the Perfect Pickle Company. His driver let him out. He went inside, sliding along the pale tan walls, matching them perfectly.

LABORATORIES said a sign on a door. Chameleon opened it. He saw tables and bottles and jars. There were tubs of pickles everywhere.

"This must be where they make the formula," he said. He waited next to a tub.

Soon a scientist in a long white coat came in. His beard was pale orange. It hung down to his buttons. "Now that I have the Pleasant Pickle formula," he wheezed, "The Pleasant Pickle Company will soon go out of business! Hee, hee, hee!" He sprinkled a bit of salt in the pickle tub next to Chameleon.

"THE PERFECT PICKLE COMPANY WILL MAKE MILLIONS!" he shouted. "MILLIONS!"

"Good heavens!" said his assistant, coming in the door. "Is anything wrong?"

"WRONG?" roared the scientist. "HOW CAN ANYTHING BE WRONG, YOU BOTTLE BRAIN! WE HAVE THE FORMULA!"

"Where is it?" asked his assistant.

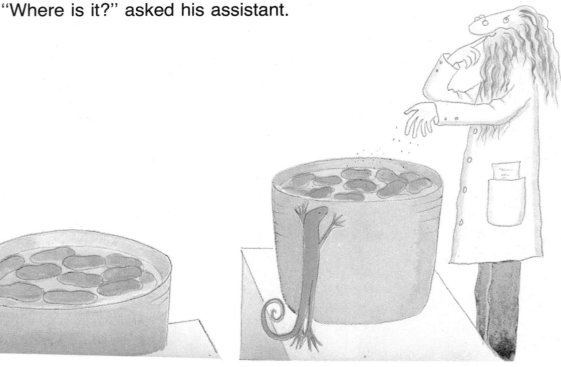

"Here!" said the scientist, flinging it down on the table. "No one else shall ever see it!"

Chameleon slid around the pickle tub. He could see the formula. It was next to the scientist's hand. He turned his skin white as the table and crept slowly out. The scientist reached for the formula. Chameleon slipped underneath it and clung to the top.

"What's this?" said the scientist, turning the paper over.

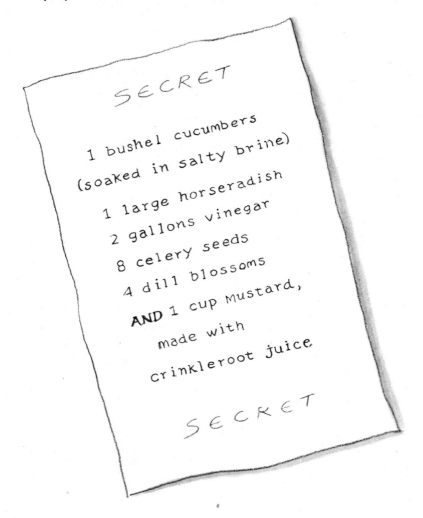

SECRET

1 bushel cucumbers
(soaked in salty brine)

1 large horseradish
2 gallons vinegar
8 celery seeds
4 dill blossoms
AND 1 cup mustard,
made with
crinkleroot juice

SECRET

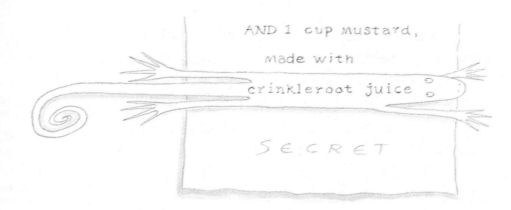

AND 1 cup mustard,
made with
crinkleroot juice
SECRET

Chameleon flipped over to the front side, and the formula fell to the table, CLUNK! Chameleon slid to the bottom and lay still. His skin matched the words underneath him perfectly.

"Crinkleroot juice," they said.

"WAIT!" snapped the scientist, staring at the page. "Eyes are looking out of the formula!"

"Eyes?" said his assistant.

"Quiet, lettucehead! I must get to the bottom of this!" His hand closed over Chameleon. Chameleon turned green as a pickle.

"AHA!" cried the scientist, holding Chameleon by the tail. "What have we here?"

"It's a pickle," said the assistant.

"It's a frog," said the scientist.

"I'm a chameleon," said Chameleon.

"WHAT," roared the scientist, "are you doing here?"

"Just looking around," said Chameleon. He stared at the formula beneath him as he swung back and forth.

"You were reading the secret formula!" said the scientist. "YOU ARE A SPY!"

Chameleon twisted loose and leaped to the table. He snatched the secret formula up and jumped down to the floor.

"WHERE IS HE?" shouted the scientist.

"He's crawling out the door," said the assistant.

"AFTER HIM!" cried the scientist. "HE MUST NOT ESCAPE!"

Chameleon ran down the hall. The door at the end said PICKLING PLANT. He hurried inside. There were tubs of pickles everywhere, pickles steaming in brine. Chameleon ran up a ramp. He could see the conveyer belts below with bottles riding along them. The bottles were passing under a chute which filled them up with pickles.

220

"STOP HIM!" shouted the scientist, rushing through the door.

Chameleon leaped to the pickle chute. But his foot slipped. Down, down, down he fell. PLUNK! into a bottle. Pickles poured down from the pickle chute.

"HELP!" yelled Chameleon.

Pickles surrounded him, and one lay on his head. The formula sank to the bottom.

"HELP! HELP!"

CLAMP! went the lid on the bottle. SWUP! went the label in front.

"HELP! HELP!" yelled Chameleon inside the bottle.

But no one heard him. Chameleon rode down the conveyer belt. He pushed up his lid just a crack.

"Number 936,073,492," said the checker at the end of the line.

Chameleon waved his arms. But his bottle moved into a box with eleven other bottles, all filled with pickles. The box lid came down, FLUMP! It was very dark.

"I'm not a pickle," said Chameleon to himself. "I'm a chameleon." He settled himself on top of a pickle and dozed in the darkness.

After a very long time, Chameleon felt himself tipping back and forth. The pickles bumped against him, and the pickle juice sloshed against his chin. "We're moving somewhere," he said.

THUMP! Creeeet, creeeet, pop! The box lid came off, letting bright daylight in. Chameleon covered his eyes. It was much too bright to see.

Slosh! Slosh! went the pickle juice. The pickles bumped his sides. CLUNK! CLUNK! Then everything was still.

Chameleon uncovered his eyes. He saw rows and rows of cans and jars, sitting on long shelves. "Where am I?" he said.

An old man passed him, pushing a basket. He stopped in front of the pickles.

"I'm in a market!" cried Chameleon. He waved his arms and pounded on the glass. But the old man didn't see or hear him. He pushed his basket slowly away.

"I could wait on this shelf for months before someone buys me!" Chameleon bit off a piece of pickle and chewed it slowly, thinking.

"I'll turn bright red," he said. "<u>Then</u> someone's sure to notice me." He turned his skin crimson and moved about, waving his arms.

"Mommy," said a little girl. "Look at that funny pickle."

"What pickle?" said her mother, reading her market list. She picked up Chameleon's jar and dropped it into her basket.

"Saved at last!" said Chameleon. A large bag of noodles lay over his jar.

"Pickles and noodles," said her mother. "Now we can go to the checkout counter."

They moved quickly to the front of the store.

"Next," said the manager.

Chameleon's jar sat on the counter. The clerk picked it up. Chameleon waved and smiled.

"WHAT'S THAT?" cried the little girl's mother.

"GOOD HEAVENS!" shouted the manager. "I'LL CALL THE FOOD INSPECTOR!"

Literary Unit

The food inspector arrived in a rush. "A CONTAMINATED BOTTLE OF PICKLES!" he announced. "THIS BOTTLE IS NOT FIT FOR HUMAN CONSUMPTION! IT SHALL BE CONDEMNED!"

"Let me out!" shouted Chameleon.

But no one heard him. The photographers came from the paper. They photographed Chameleon's jar. Someone put the jar in a bag and carried it off to the police station.

"PERFECT PICKLE COMPANY CLOSED!" said the papers the next day. "A CONTAMINATED JAR OF PICKLES IS FOUND ON A MARKET SHELF. THE PUBLIC IS OUTRAGED."

"Good heavens!" said Chameleon's mother when she saw the paper that morning. She hurried to town.

"LET MY SON OUT OF THAT JAR!" she said.

The police chief pried off the lid.

"Thank you," said Chameleon, dripping pickle juice over the desk. He followed his mother out the door and hurried home.

"Chameleon," said his mother at breakfast, "how did you like your new job?"

"It was all right," said Chameleon, "if you like being a pickle."

The telephone rang.

"Hello?" answered Chameleon.

It was the president of the Pleasant Pickle Company. "I've read the morning paper," he said. "Good work!"

"Thank you," said Chameleon.

"Did you get the formula?"

"Yes," said Chameleon.

"YAHOOOOOOOOOOO!" yelled the president into the receiver.

"I'll be right there," said Chameleon.

He hurried down to 222 South Bean Street. Before he could knock, the door opened.

"THERE HE IS!" shouted the members of the company. They carried Chameleon into the banquet room. Balloons hung from the ceiling.

"Where is the formula?" asked the president.

Chameleon held up the wrinkled paper. "Here it is!" he said proudly. Everyone clapped.

"I'll copy it on the blackboard," said the president. "Let me have it."

He started to read out loud, and stopped. "GOOD HEAVENS!" he shouted. "The writing at the bottom is blurred. The last ingredient is missing!"

"MISSING?" cried everyone.

"The secret formula is worthless without it!" groaned the president. "What shall we do?"

"WAIT!" cried Chameleon. He grabbed the secret formula and lay across the bottom where the last line had been. Spots and swirls flickered over his back. Dots and dashes flashed on and off. Then, all at once, two words appeared in large clear letters:

"THAT'S IT!" shouted the president. "Chameleon has saved our formula!"

"HOORAY for Chameleon!" yelled everyone.

The president wrote "crinkleroot juice" on the blackboard while everyone cheered. Then he presented Chameleon with a gold plaque. It said:

For CHAMELEON, THE PERFECT SPY
with thanks from THE PLEASANT PICKLE COMPANY
Makers of THE WORLD'S BEST PICKLES

Comprehension Check

1. What was Chameleon's special talent?
2. How do you think Chameleon felt when he was trapped in the pickle jar?
3. Why do you suppose the writing at the bottom of the formula was blurred at the end of the story?
4. If you had been hired to recover the stolen pickle formula, how would you have done it?

Hiding

by Dorothy Aldis

I'm hiding, I'm hiding,
And no one knows where;
For all they can see is my
Toes and my hair.

"Have you looked in the INKWELL?"
And Mother said, "Where?"
"In the INKWELL," said Father. But
I was not there.

"Inside the mirror's
A pretty good place,"
Said Father and looked, but saw
Only his face.

Then I laughed out loud
And I wiggled my toes
And Father said—"Look, dear,
I wonder if those

Toes could be Benny's
There are ten of them. See?"
And they WERE SO surprised to find
Out it was me!

Problems and Solutions

Sometimes a character in a story has a problem to solve. Read the story that follows. What problem does Irving have? What do you think about his solution?

Irving wanted to ride a bicycle more than anything else in the world. He imagined himself racing like the wind down Hinkle Street. But Irving had one little problem. He was afraid to get on his bike.

Then one day Irving had an idea. The bike scared him because it was so big. So maybe he could do something to make the bike smaller. Irving put blocks on the pedals. He lowered the handlebars. He lowered the seat. Then he took a deep breath and hopped on. His legs worked the pedals and the bike began to move.

"I'm riding! I'm really riding!" he shouted, as he headed for Hinkle Street.

Irving's problem was that he was afraid to ride his bicycle. He thought the bike was too big for him. What did Irving do to solve his problem?

Irving made the bike seem smaller than it really was. Tell about the things that Irving did to make his bike seem smaller.

Do you think Irving's solution was a good one? Let's look at other ways Irving might have solved his problem.

Irving could have asked his parents to buy him a smaller bike. Do you think that would have been a good solution? Would it have been fair for Irving to ask his parents to buy him a new bike when he already had one?

Irving could have put his bike away until he had grown taller. Do you think that would have been a good solution? How long might Irving have had to wait before he could ride his bike?

Of all the possible solutions, Irving's seems like the best one. His solution helped him to ride his bike right away.

Practice

Read the following story about a problem and a solution. Then answer the questions.

Myra saw a big, empty wooden box near the park. She thought it would make a wonderful house for Chip, her dog. Now all she had to do was get it home.

Myra grabbed the box around the middle. She tried to lift it, but the box was too heavy. She tried to push the box, but it wouldn't move an inch.

Just then Myra saw some friends who were playing baseball. She ran over to them and asked if they would help her. After the game, Myra and her friends moved the box to her backyard. Now Myra's dog, Chip, has a wonderful doghouse.

1. What was Myra's problem? How did she solve it?
2. What are some other things Myra could have done to solve her problem?
3. Do you think Myra's solution was a good one? Why or why not?

As you read the next story, "The Ultimate Auto," decide if the characters find a good solution to their problem.

The Ultimate Auto

by Patrick McGivern

The mayor of the city of New York was dictating a letter one day. Then all of a sudden, she looked up with a funny expression on her face and fell out of her chair.

"What's the matter?" said the mayor's worried secretary, helping his boss to her feet.

"I just had a feeling," the mayor said, shaking. "I just had the feeling that the Ultimate Auto has arrived in my city. The Ultimate Auto —you know what that means."

"I don't know what you're talking about," said the secretary, brushing some red tape off the mayor's suit.

"Just look outside," the mayor said, leading her secretary to a window. "What do you see?"

"Just a lot of parked cars."

"Those cars aren't parked," the mayor pointed out. "They're inching forward—maybe twelve inches a minute. That's moving. That's what traffic in this city is like every day. But when the Ultimate Auto gets to town—and we've been expecting it for years—it will be just one car too many. The Ultimate Auto will jam in that traffic like a key in a lock. Everything in the city will come to a halt. We'll have the biggest traffic jam in history. I have nightmares about it. I even have daymares. And now I've got this crazy feeling that the Ultimate Auto is here."

234

The mayor's crazy feeling was right. Indeed, the Ultimate Auto had already entered New York. It was a funny little blue car. The driver was Samuel Smerb, a kennel worker for the Columbia County Humane Society in upstate New York.

Back at the dog pound, they were running low on Vitamin Compound Z for the dogs. Smerb was driving to Manhattan to pick up a new supply. To make the trip more bearable, Smerb took some of his four-footed friends.

Smerb swung onto Fifth Avenue and headed the Ultimate Auto into a space between a big truck and a bus. It was just the right size for his funny little car. But the space kept getting smaller and smaller. Then the truck stopped and the bus stopped. Smerb stopped too. So did the taxicab behind him. In fact, everything in every direction came to a stop.

Hours went by. Smerb wished the taxi driver behind him would stop yelling and shaking his fist. It began to grow dark and still nothing moved. So Smerb decided to walk his four-footed friends.

Outside, he saw a police officer and asked what was going on.

"It looks as if the Ultimate Auto has arrived in New York City," said Patrol Officer Michael Calzone of The Bronx, New York.

"What's an Ultimate Auto?" asked Smerb.

"You'll find out tonight," said Calzone, "when the mayor goes on television."

"I don't have a TV in the car," said Smerb.

"Well, in that case, you can watch at my house," said Calzone.

"Thank you very much," replied Smerb.

That evening, when the mayor appeared on television, Smerb watched from Officer Calzone's house in The Bronx.

"Friends," the mayor began, "the traffic situation in our city is . . . well, it's completely out of control."

The mayor went on to explain what had happened and declared that a citywide emergency would be in effect until the Ultimate Auto was found.

"Our entire police force will be looking for the car," the mayor continued. "Helicopters and planes will join in the search from the air. I promise you, we will do everything in our power to get the traffic moving again. As a first step in this direction, no more tickets will be given for speeding. And you may be pleased to know that I have fired the Commissioner of Traffic."

The next morning Smerb and his friends went back to their car. The taxi driver was still there, shaking his fist.

That night the mayor went on television again. She said that the search for the Ultimate Auto had been narrowed down to Manhattan.

"We are still doing everything in our power to get things moving again," she added. "And as one more step in this direction, I have ordered that all traffic signals stop flashing red. So all cars in the city have a green light to go, uh, when they get a chance."

Then the mayor's face darkened. In a voice that could hardly be heard, she said, "At the request of the City Council, I will not seek reelection in November."

238

Smerb watched the mayor with the Calzones. Then he told everyone what had happened to <u>him</u> as he turned onto Fifth Avenue.

"What!" exclaimed Officer Calzone. "Say that again."

"I wedged in between the truck and the bus. Then I stopped, and the taxi behind me stopped. I was jammed in like a key in a lock. Say, why are you turning green?"

Calzone jumped to the telephone and quickly dialed the mayor's private number.

"I may be wrong," he said, turning to Smerb, "and I may get fired. But I'm going to tell the mayor that the Ultimate Auto is <u>yours</u>!"

Smerb fainted. So did his four-footed friends.

On the following day the scene around the Ultimate Auto was not to be believed. Everyone was there, from Smerb and Officer Calzone to the mayor. A crowd of about twelve thousand people was also on the scene. So were about one hundred radio and television reporters.

Suddenly every camera, every microphone, and every face turned toward the mayor.

"Your Honor," said a reporter. "We all know that you have found the Ultimate Auto. But traffic is still stuck. So can you tell us how you are going to get it moving again?"

The mayor's smile fell at her feet. She turned to the new Commissioner of Traffic. "I think you can answer that, eh, Bob?" she said.

The Commissioner of Traffic turned to the Commissioner of Police. "This seems to be your job, eh, Charlie?" he said.

The Commissioner of Police turned to Patrol Officer Calzone. "Well, Lieutenant Calzone," he said. "You found the Ultimate Auto. Now what are you going to do about the traffic jam?"

"I . . . uh . . . well," stammered Calzone.

Before Calzone could finish his statement, that angry taxi driver jumped in. "If it were up to me," he said, "I would take this guy's Ultimate Auto and break it up into little pieces and—"

"And mail the pieces back to Smerb," said Lieutenant Calzone. "Just as I was about to say. If we take the Ultimate Auto apart, then traffic can move again. It's as easy as taking a key out of a lock."

Everyone cheered, everyone except Smerb, that is.

"Look," he told everybody, "you can mail the pieces of my car back to me. That'll be fine. But I've still got to pick up that vitamin compound and get back to the dog pound. How do I do that?"

"Why, in my police helicopter," the mayor said quickly.

When the cheering died down, the mayor told everyone that she had changed her mind about not running for office again. Now she was ready to be mayor for four more years.

That sounds like the end of the story, but it isn't.

The mayor let Smerb keep the helicopter until all the pieces of the Ultimate Auto arrived in the mail. But somebody had made a mistake. The car's engine was delivered to Samuel Smerb of Columbia County, New Mexico. When the real Smerb told the mayor this, there was only one thing she could do.

"OK," she said. "You can keep my helicopter. But do me one favor. Stay out of town!"

Smerb does just that. If you ever get up to Columbia County, you may see him. When he isn't working at the dog pound, Smerb still takes his four-footed friends for rides. Now he does it in an official New York City helicopter. Sometimes Lieutenant Calzone and his family go along too.

Comprehension Check

1. Why was Samuel Smerb driving into Manhattan?
2. Look up the word ultimate in the glossary at the back of your book. Then tell why you think this story is called "The Ultimate Auto."
3. Do you think it was a good idea for the mayor to send out helicopters and planes to search for the Ultimate Auto? Why or why not?
4. Do you think what happened in "The Ultimate Auto" could really happen? Why or why not?

Skill Check

Answer the questions below about the story you just read.

1. What was the problem facing the mayor of the City of New York?
2. How did the mayor try to solve the problem?
3. Tell why her solutions did or did not work.
4. What was Officer Calzone's solution to the problem?
5. Tell why his solution did or did not work.
6. If you were the mayor, how would you have solved the problem?

The Bicycle
and How It Works

adapted from a book by
David Inglis Urquhart

    The year was 1816. There were no airplanes, no trains, and no cars. How did people get around? They walked, they rode on the backs of animals, or they used wagons or carriages. Then one day Baron Karl Drais von Sauerbronn of Germany got tired of touring his land on foot or by carriage. He wanted a new and easier way to get around. So what did he do? He invented the bicycle.

    The baron's bicycle was an immediate success. Within a few years, it began to be used in many different countries. But back then, a bicycle wasn't cheap. Believe it or not, in the 1800s, a bicycle cost the same as what $2,400 is in today's money. It took many years to develop a bicycle that was inexpensive enough for most people to buy.

Have you ever thought about how a bicycle is put together? Have you ever wondered how it works?

A bicycle looks as though it is just a simple metal frame joining two wheels, with handlebars at the front and pedals. Each part may seem simple, but making it all work together took a lot of effort and a lot of thought. A frame without wheels would be useless because it wouldn't move. Wheels without brakes would be dangerous and difficult to stop. Brakes, wheels, and a frame without handlebars would be impossible to steer. Each part of the bicycle is important for the role it plays in the way the whole machine works.

246

The frame of a bicycle holds all its parts together, much as your skeleton holds the parts of your body together. The frame should be both as strong and as light as possible.

The first bicycle frame was made of wood. It held together two wheels, which were also made of wood. Later steel and aluminum frames replaced the wood frames. But steel was too heavy and aluminum was not strong enough. Finally, hollow steel was used as a frame. It was strong, it would not bend, and it weighed very little. So far hollow steel has proved to be the best material with which to make bicycle frames.

Did you know that today most bicycles weigh about thirty pounds? Racing bicycles weigh even less. But years ago, bicycles weighed sixty pounds or more.

We've seen what a bicycle frame is made of. But a bicycle can't go very far with just a frame. It needs wheels.

Take a look at the picture below. Do you see the hub? The hub is the center of the wheel. Do you see the axle? The axle is a metal bar inside the hub. The wheel turns on the axle. Do you see the rim of the wheel? The rim is the outside part of the wheel. It holds the rubber tire in place.

Now look at the spokes. The spokes are thin metal rods that connect the rim to the hub of the wheel. Spokes make the wheel stronger.

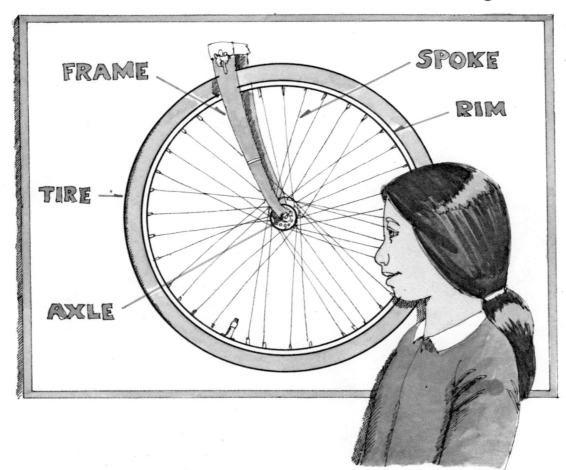

FRAME

SPOKE

RIM

TIRE

AXLE

In early days, wheels were made of wood
and rimmed with iron. Imagine how uncomfortable
that would be to ride on! These kinds of wheels
could not absorb the bumps on road surfaces. In
fact, bicycles that had these wooden wheels were
called "boneshakers." That's because when you
rode one of these bikes, you felt as though your
bones were shaking.

Old-time tires weren't comfortable to ride on
either. They were very hard. They were made of
solid rubber. Then in 1888 rubber tires filled
with air were invented. This type of tire is still
used today. Air-filled tires are a great deal
more comfortable to ride on. They are able to
"give" with the road surface. This means they
form an air cushion. The air cushion makes the
ride smoother.

Now we have a frame and wheels on our bicycle. But how do we make the bike move?

When you ride a bicycle, you propel it with your feet by using a set of pedals. The very first bicycle had no pedals. It was a combination scooter and bicycle. A heavy wooden frame was placed on two wheels. The rider sat on a kind of saddle and pushed the bicycle along by foot.

Then finally, in 1839, a way of attaching pedals to the front wheel was discovered. Each time the pedals made a complete turn, the front wheel would go around once. The larger the front wheel, the faster the bicycle could go.

Pedaling the bicycle was much better than pushing it along the road by foot. But there was still a limit to how fast it could move. Speed depended on how fast the rider could pedal and how large the front wheel was.

As bicycle riders wanted to go faster and faster, new methods of propelling the bicycle had to be found. Look at the illustration below. You'll see two bicycles. The one in picture A is an old-time bicycle. It has pedals attached to its large front wheel.

The bicycle in picture B is a modern one. It has pedals attached to its frame, between the front wheel and the back wheel. There's also a chain attached to the frame.

On the old-time bicycle, the pedals turn the wheel. On the modern bicycle, the pedals turn the chain and the chain turns the wheel.

We have our bicycle moving now. We can even go pretty fast. But how do we slow down or stop? We use our brakes.

Most bicycles today have one of two kinds of brakes: hand brakes or foot brakes. Hand brakes are operated by squeezing levers on the handlebars of the bicycle.

Foot brakes are worked by the rider's feet. The brakes are located in the hub of the rear wheel. To stop a bike with foot brakes, you must backpedal.

252

Now when we ride our bicycle, we can slow down and stop. But how do we get the bike to go in the right direction? We do this by steering.

Steering is a simple process. The front wheel of the bicycle is controlled from the handlebars. It turns when the handlebars are turned. This means a rider can change direction by moving the handlebars.

In the past, many different styles and kinds of bicycles were sold. There were bicycles built for two, three, and even more. There was even one bicycle called an "ordinary." It was five feet high. Today we still have regular bicycles and bicycles built for two. We even have a kind of "ordinary" called the *unicycle.* The unicycle has only one wheel. It's quite a trick to stay on one!

Now more than ever bicycling is popular all over the country. Certain cities have opened up bicycle lanes. Some cities even close their public parks to all other traffic during certain hours of the day. In many parts of the country, bicycle paths and trails are already in use. Plans for new ones are now underway in many national and state parks.

Why all this interest in bicycling? Well, bicycling is an excellent form of exercise. It's an inexpensive way of traveling because you don't need to use fuel. It doesn't cause pollution problems. And, as most of you will agree, it's great fun!

254

Comprehension Check

1. In what year was the bicycle invented? By whom?
2. Name the different parts of a bicycle.
3. Why do you think old-time bicycles were so much heavier than modern ones?
4. Do you think moving the pedals from the front wheel to the frame of the bicycle was a good idea? Why or why not?
5. If you know how to ride a bicycle, tell how you learned. If you don't know how to ride a bicycle, tell why you would or would not like to learn.

Skill Check

Read the following paragraph. Then answer the questions that follow.

Now more than ever bicycling is popular all over the country. Certain cities have opened up bicycle lanes. Some cities even close their public parks to all other traffic during certain hours of the day. In many parts of the country, bicycle paths and trails are already in use. Plans for new ones are underway in many national and state parks.

1. Which sentence in this paragraph tells the main idea?
2. Which sentences tell details about the main idea?

Figures of Speech

Sometimes the words we use don't mean exactly what they say. Read the story that follows and see if you can find some examples of this.

"My cat Rupert is a crazy cat," said Wanda. "He gobbles his food like a pig. Then he speeds around the house like a rocket. He is as big as a tiger and his coat is orange. I think he looks like a pumpkin."

What do you think Wanda means when she says that Rupert speeds around the house like a rocket? Can Rupert really move as fast as a rocket? Does he travel to other planets?

When Wanda said Rupert moves like a rocket, she used a figure of speech. A **figure of speech** is a colorful way to compare two things. Rupert doesn't really move like a rocket. But there is something about the way Rupert moves that makes Wanda compare him to a rocket. Can you guess what it is?

Wanda says that Rupert is like a rocket when he runs around the house. You know that rockets move very fast. If Rupert is like a rocket, then he must be a very fast runner.

Wanda says Rupert eats like a pig. Why do you think Wanda compares Rupert to a pig? Use the story to help you decide. What other figures of speech does Wanda use to describe Rupert?

What does Wanda compare Rupert to in the paragraph below? Can you find the figure of speech she uses?

"Rupert doesn't like to get wet. He wants me to think he can't swim. But I know that he is a fish in the water."

Wanda says that Rupert is a fish. Of course, you know that Rupert isn't really a fish. Wanda is using a figure of speech again.

What do you know about fish? Are they very good swimmers? If Rupert is a fish in the water, what kind of swimmer is he?

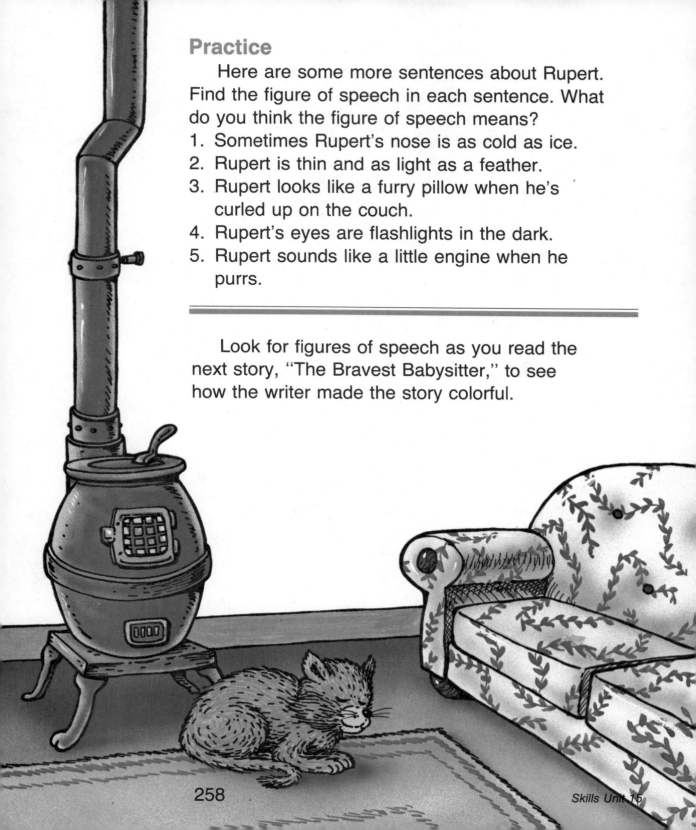

Practice

Here are some more sentences about Rupert. Find the figure of speech in each sentence. What do you think the figure of speech means?

1. Sometimes Rupert's nose is as cold as ice.
2. Rupert is thin and as light as a feather.
3. Rupert looks like a furry pillow when he's curled up on the couch.
4. Rupert's eyes are flashlights in the dark.
5. Rupert sounds like a little engine when he purrs.

Look for figures of speech as you read the next story, "The Bravest Babysitter," to see how the writer made the story colorful.

The Bravest Babysitter

by Barbara Greenberg

The doorbell rang, and Lisa galloped over to help Mother open the door. Heather, Lisa's favorite babysitter, walked in. Heather bent down and said, "Hi, Lis. You got a haircut. Now I can tickle you right here on the back of your neck."

"What do you have on?" asked Lisa. She opened Heather's coat. Heather had come right from hockey practice. Under her long coat she wore shorts. Purple and orange stripes chased each other around her knee socks.

Lisa always had a good time with Heather. Heather liked to read books aloud, and she laughed hard at the silly parts and made her voice spooky for the scary parts. She was good at drawing, and she called Lisa "Lis."

Mother left, and Lisa and Heather got to work on a collage. Lisa liked to paste bumpy and smooth and bright-colored things all together on paper to make a design. This time she got big macaroni and small macaroni and some white buttons and brown buttons and a big shiny gold one. Heather cut out pictures from a magazine.

It started raining while they were working on the collage. It was an angry, windy rain. It beat against the house and rattled the windows.

Suddenly the darkness outside got white with light. Then thunder began to rumble through the sky like loud firecrackers.

"Oh, no. Thunder!" said Heather. She put down the scissors and held onto the arms of the chair. "Get ready. Here comes another one," she said after the next flash of lightning.

"What's the matter, Heather?" asked Lisa. "Are you scared?"

"Scared? Who's scared of a little thunder?" said Heather when it was quiet again. "Now listen, you thunder, you'll have to whisper, please," yelled Heather.

Lisa laughed.

"Oh, no. Here comes more thunder," said Heather. And she put her hands over her ears and squeezed her eyes shut.

"My mother always tells me to keep busy so I don't think so much about the thunder," Lisa said. "So let's paste."

Lisa pasted her big macaroni and small macaroni and her white buttons and brown buttons and her big shiny gold buttons on some paper. She loved sticking her fingers in the paste and making collages, and she didn't think about the thunder.

But Heather wasn't paying attention to what she was doing. She pasted a picture right onto the table instead of onto the paper.

"Oh, no," said Lisa. "Look what you did!"

"Maybe we ought to eat supper now," said Heather.

"OK," said Lisa. "And let's play restaurant."

They had hamburgers on buns and apple juice with straws—just like at Dan's Diner in town.

While she was eating her hamburger, Lisa said, "Let's make believe I'm the waitress and you're the little girl."

She patted Heather on the head and said, "Now you eat up all that good hamburger, honey. Don't spill the sugar on the floor or we'll get ants."

"What did you say?" asked Heather.

Heather hadn't heard a word, and she hadn't eaten a bite.

"Let's think of something else to do," said Lisa. "Do you want to read me a story?"

Lisa and Heather snuggled together in the soft armchair in the living room. Heather read a story.

There was a blaze of lightning and a bang of thunder. Heather sank lower into the chair and pulled Lisa down with her. Heather went on reading, but she didn't laugh now at the silly parts or make her voice spooky for the scary parts. She read and then looked out of the window, and then read again and looked out of the window again. She kept losing her place.

264

"Let's play dress-up instead," said Lisa at
last. They went up to her room. Then she dragged
out her box full of old clothes. She draped a
shawl around her shoulders, and she put a floppy
hat, piled high with cherries and feathers, on
her head. She pulled out a long dress and gave
it to Heather.

But Heather got all tangled up in the dress.
First she put one arm where the head should go.
Then she put her head where the arm should go.
Finally she put it on right.

Then Lisa pulled out a pair of shoes and gave
them to Heather. But Heather put the shoes on
the wrong feet.

266

There was another flash of light. Then *rumble, roar, crash* went the thunder.

"That was a loud one," said Heather.

"It will stop soon," said Lisa.

"You're brave, Lis," said Heather.

"Let's go downstairs and draw with crayons," said Lisa. They changed back into their own clothes. Then they hurried downstairs.

Lisa drew a picture of a sunny day with red and yellow flowers and green stems, and a big, round, orange sun. Heather drew a picture of a rainstorm with a streak of lightning across the sky.

"I like yours better," said Heather.

"Here. It's for you," said Lisa.

It was Lisa's bedtime. She put on her pajamas and got ready for bed. But Heather said, "You may stay up tonight until the rain stops. Let's keep each other company a little while longer."

"Sometimes when there's thunder outside, my mother puts on a record and we dance," Lisa said.

Lisa and Heather chose a record and played it loud. Heather loved to dance. She moved up and down and around like a pretty pony on a carousel. As she danced, her long hair flapped against her back.

Lisa danced like a playful kitten. She hopped and jumped and tumbled on the floor. But she couldn't get her short hair to flap like Heather's.

When the record was over, Heather said, "Look, it's stopped raining. There's no more thunder. You'd better go to sleep now. Would you like me to tuck you in?"

"No," said Lisa. "I'll tuck myself in tonight."

"You're a very good babysitter, Lis," said Heather.

"I know," said Lisa. "I hope there's thunder the next time you come, so I can take care of you again. I like being a babysitter."

Comprehension Check

1. Why was Heather Lisa's favorite babysitter?
2. Why do you think Lisa wanted to put on a record and dance?
3. At the end of the story, Heather says Lisa is a good babysitter. Do you think Lisa was a good babysitter? Why or why not?
4. Would you like to be a babysitter someday? Why or why not?

Skill Check

The sentences below are from the story you just read. Find the figure of speech in each sentence. Then tell what you think each figure of speech means.

1. Then thunder began to rumble through the sky like loud firecrackers.
2. She moved up and down and around like a pretty pony on a carousel.
3. Lisa danced like a playful kitten.

The Case of the Broken Globe

by Donald J. Sobol

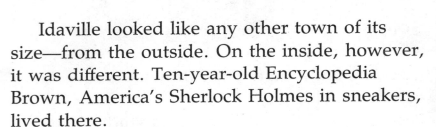

Idaville looked like any other town of its size—from the outside. On the inside, however, it was different. Ten-year-old Encyclopedia Brown, America's Sherlock Holmes in sneakers, lived there.

Encyclopedia's father was Chief of Police. People said he was the smartest Chief of Police in the world and his officers were the best trained and the bravest. Chief Brown knew better.

His men were brave, true enough. They did their jobs well. But Chief Brown brought his hardest cases home for Encyclopedia to solve.

The Browns were sitting in the living room after dinner one evening when Mr. Morton dropped by. Mr. Morton taught at the high school. He and Chief Brown had been friends since boyhood.

"I hate to bother you at this hour," apologized Mr. Morton. "But . . . well, something serious happened in my class today. And," he added, "I need your help . . . er . . . as a friend."

"I understand," said Chief Brown. "You want to keep the trouble quiet."

"Yes," replied Mr. Morton. "My students aren't criminals. And to tell the truth, no law was broken."

"I promise not to make any arrests, if that's what's worrying you," said Chief Brown with a grin. "Now, what is this all about?"

"I gave my class a test today," said Mr. Morton. "I left the room for five minutes. While I was gone, a globe of the world, worth ninety dollars, was smashed."

"And you want me to find out who broke it?" asked Chief Brown.

"I do," said Mr. Morton. "I doubt if it was knocked over on purpose. More likely it was an accident. However, no one in the class will tell me who broke it."

272

"What was the test you gave the class?" asked Mrs. Brown.

"It was on caption writing," answered Mr. Morton. "Each student was given six pictures and told to write a caption—a description—for each."

Mr. Morton opened his briefcase. He pulled out the test papers and showed them to Chief Brown. Chief Brown looked at them quickly and handed them to Mrs. Brown. She gave each a glance and passed them to Encyclopedia.

While the grown-ups talked about the case, the boy detective gave the tests his full attention. Each student had been given the same pictures to work with. The difference in what each wrote was remarkable.

One of the test papers, turned in by a boy named Gene Dickman, caught Encyclopedia's eye. All the other students had written captions of twenty to fifty words, but Gene had written only one word under each picture.

Under a picture of a clock with both hands pointing to 12, he had written "NOON."

Under a picture of an old sea captain scanning the horizon with a spyglass, he had written "SEES."

Under a picture of a screen with white dots, he had written "RADAR."

Under a picture of a calm and unrippled lake, he had written "LEVEL."

Under a picture of a paperhanger working on a wall, he had written "REPAPER."

"I wonder . . ." Encyclopedia muttered.

274

Hurriedly he checked the names at the top of the other test papers: Robert Mason, Mary Keith, Anna McGill, George Worth, Mike Duval, Phil Johnson, Connie Logan, Scott Mucie, and Dwight Sherman.

Encyclopedia closed his eyes. He always closed his eyes when he did his heaviest thinking. Then he asked a question. One question was all he needed to ask in order to solve a case.

"Are these all the students in your class, Mr. Morton?"

"Yes, it's a small class," answered the teacher. "There are three girls and seven boys."

Suddenly Mr. Morton frowned. He had noticed Gene Dickman's test paper on top of the pile on Encyclopedia's lap.

"I don't understand what happened to Gene," said Mr. Morton. "He is my brightest student, and yet he failed. He wrote only one word under each picture!"

"Perhaps he didn't have time to write more," said Chief Brown, "because he broke the globe."

Mr. Morton shook his head. "I left the classroom right after giving out the tests. I was gone only five minutes. Gene and everyone else had plenty of time to finish the test before the period ended."

"I thought you tried to find out who broke the globe," said Chief Brown. "Didn't that take time?"

"No," replied Mr. Morton, "I didn't notice the broken globe till the bell rang. I held the class a few minutes, but nobody confessed."

"It's a tough case," admitted Chief Brown. "There is no telling which boy is guilty."

"Maybe the guilty person is a girl," said Mrs. Brown.

"You're both right," said Encyclopedia. "A boy and a girl are guilty."

Literary Unit

For a moment the room was quiet. The grownups stared in amazement at the boy detective.

"Leroy," said his mother. "How do you know that?"

"I learned it from Gene Dickman," replied Encyclopedia.

"You spoke with Gene?" gasped Mr. Morton.

"No, I read his test," replied Encyclopedia. "The way I see it, Gene didn't want to be called a squealer. But neither did he like seeing the guilty boy and girl refuse to own up to what they did."

"I don't understand a word," protested Mr. Morton.

"Gene used the test to name the guilty boy and girl," explained Encyclopedia.

HOW

(*Turn to the next page for the solution to "The Case of the Broken Globe."*)

Solution to The Case of the Broken Globe

Gene Dickman had written only one word to describe each picture in the test: NOON, SEES, RADAR, LEVEL, and REPAPER.

The five words were the clue. Each was a *palindrome*; that is, a word that reads the same backward and forward.

Two students, Encyclopedia saw, had names that were palindromes. They were ANNA McGill and Robert—BOB—Mason.

The next day Mr. Morton questioned only Anna and Bob about the broken globe. They thought he had positive proof of their guilt, so they confessed. After he had left the classroom during the test, they had clowned around and had knocked over the globe.

Comprehension Check

1. Why did Mr. Morton go to see Chief Brown?
2. Why do you think Encyclopedia asked Mr. Morton if the students whose test papers he saw were the only ones in the class?
3. Do you think the clues Gene Dickman left were good ones? Why or why not?
4. As the story explains, a *palindrome* is a word that reads the same backward and forward, like *tot* or *pep*. See how many palindromes you can think of.

Literary Unit

When I Grow Up

by William Wise

When I grow up,
I think I'll be
A detective
With a skeleton key.
I could be a soldier
And a sailor too;
I'd like to be a keeper
At the public zoo.

I'll own a trumpet
And I'll play a tune;
I'll keep a spaceship
To explore the moon.

I'd like to be the driver
On a diesel train;
And it must be fun
To run a building crane.

I'll live in a lighthouse
And guard the shore;
And I know I'll want to be
A dozen things more.

For the more a child lives
The more a child learns—
I think I'll be all of them
By taking turns.

Kitchen Window Gardens

by Katherine N. Cutler

Did you know that the plants you see in this kitchen window garden grew from fruits and vegetables you can find in your supermarket? What kinds of vegetables and fruits are they? They are avocados, carrots, beets, and sweet potatoes. And, as you can see, they all make lovely and interesting plants.

By following the steps on the next few pages, you can grow any of these plants yourself. You might find one of these fruits or vegetables at home in your own refrigerator. If not, you can ask your mother or father to help you pick some out. Then you'll be well on your way to growing your own kitchen window garden.

Avocado Plant

Here's what you need:
1. the pit from a ripe avocado
2. 1 medium-sized drinking glass
3. 4 toothpicks

Now follow these steps.

Step One: Wash the avocado pit, and peel away any brown skin that comes off easily. Then stick the four toothpicks around the middle of the pit. If you break a toothpick, try again.

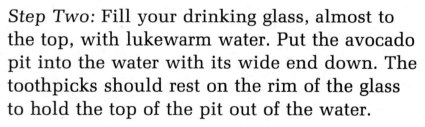

Step Two: Fill your drinking glass, almost to the top, with lukewarm water. Put the avocado pit into the water with its wide end down. The toothpicks should rest on the rim of the glass to hold the top of the pit out of the water.

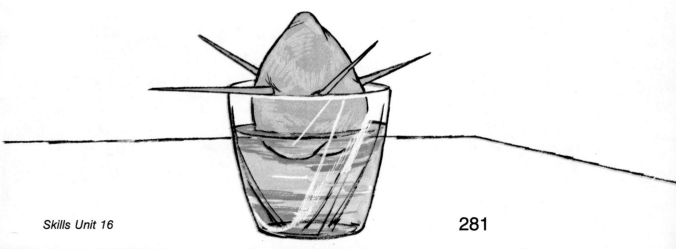

Step Three: Now look for a warm and shady place to put your plant. A kitchen cupboard or a shelf in your own room will do. From time to time you'll need to add a little water to the glass to keep the bottom of the pit covered. Check your plant every day. Soon you'll see some tiny roots appear.

Step Four: After three or four weeks, more and more roots will fill the glass. The top of the avocado pit, or seed, will split open, and inside you'll see some pale-green shoots. The strongest shoot will grow up to become the plant's main stem. The first tender leaves will sprout from its tip.

Step Five: When the plant's main stem is a little over six inches high, get your scissors and snip about three inches off the top. This will help your plant sprout side branches. Once side branches grow, the plant won't look so weak and spindly.

Step Six: Wait about two more weeks. Does your plant look strong enough to pot? If it does, put a layer of pebbles in the bottom of a planting pot. Then place a layer of soil in the pot. Next carefully put the avocado pit in. Fill the rest of the pot up with soil. Make sure all the roots are covered and the top of the pit peeks out above the soil. Now move your avocado plant to a sunny windowsill. Keep it moist, and have fun watching it grow tall and beautiful.

Sweet-Potato Vine

Here's what you need:

1. 2 sweet potatoes with lots of eyes. (Eyes are the little bumps on the skin of the potato.)
2. 2 medium-sized drinking glasses or jars
3. 8 toothpicks

Now follow these steps.

Step One: Fill the glasses up about halfway with lukewarm water. Find a sunny windowsill, and put a jar on either side of it.

Step Two: Stick in four toothpicks around the middle of each potato. Now put the potatoes into the glasses or jars so that the toothpicks hold most of the potato up out of the water. As the picture shows, only the bottom tips need to be under water.

Step Three: Check your potatoes every day. Are the bottom tips covered? If not, add a little water to the glasses. In about two weeks, you'll see little green shoots sprouting from the potato eyes. Soon a leaf will appear, and then a vine.

Step Four: Ask someone to help you attach a string or wire around the window frame. If the vines are long enough, you can gently train them to start growing up the string. To do this, carefully intertwine the vine with the string. Your sweet-potato vines will climb higher and higher. Soon you'll have a leafy green frame all around your window.

Carrot and Beet Plants

Here's what you need:

1. 2 foil pie plates
2. waterproof paint and a paintbrush
3. 1 fresh carrot
4. 1 fresh beet
5. scissors

Now follow these steps.

Step One: Paint the foil plates with your favorite colors. Add some designs if you want. Now you have some pretty containers for your carrot and beet plants.

Step Two: Take your scissors and cut the leafy part off the vegetables. Then ask someone to help you cut off the bottom of your carrot and beet. Be careful to leave about one inch on the tops of the vegetables. Now, if you're hungry, you can eat what's left of the carrot.

286

Step Three: Fill the foil plates you painted earlier with water and put in the pieces of carrot and beet. The water should come up to, but not cover, the tops of the vegetables.

Step Four: In the next few weeks, look for fresh green shoots. Keep adding water to each dish to replace the water that has evaporated.

Step Five: When the plants look leafy and strong, they can be planted in pots. Line the bottom of each pot with pebbles, then fill each with soil. Next carefully place your carrot and beet plants in the pots. Pat the soil down around the plants. Now take a look. You began both the beet and the carrot plant the same way, but notice how different they are! The carrot leaves are as delicate as a fern, while the beet has wide green leaves with reddish stems.

Comprehension Check

1. What are some of the vegetables and fruits that can be used to plant a kitchen window garden?
2. Why do you think sunny windows are a good place to keep plants?
3. Do you think growing a plant is easy or difficult? Tell why you think as you do.
4. Have you ever taken care of an indoor or outdoor garden? Tell about it.

Skill Check

Look at the sentences below. Each sentence tells one of the steps you must follow in order to grow an avocado plant. Put the steps in their correct order.

1. Fill a glass, almost to the top, with lukewarm water, and put the avocado pit into the water with its wide end down.
2. Stick four toothpicks around the middle of the pit.
3. Wash the avocado pit, and peel away any brown skin that comes off easily.
4. Find a warm and shady place to put the plant.
5. Place the avocado pit in a planting pot.
6. When the plant's main stem is a little over six inches high, snip about three inches off the top.

Understanding Story Characters

In a story the things that characters say and do help you understand their feelings and the kind of people they are.

Read the following story about Rodney Pip. See if you can figure out how he feels and what kind of person he is through his words and actions.

Rodney Pip was a magician. He could have been the best magician in the world except for one thing. His magic tricks never worked the way he wanted them to.

One time Sparky Smith asked Rodney to change his hat into a puppy. This is what happened:

"Hey!" cried Sparky. "That's not a puppy!"

"No," sighed Rodney. "It looks like a tuna-fish sandwich and a glass of milk."

"I didn't want lunch!" roared Sparky. "I wanted a puppy! You're not a magician. You're just a cook."

Poor Rodney. He couldn't seem to make anything except food. Soon everybody stopped asking him to perform his magic tricks.

"I'm a flop!" Rodney sobbed. "I'm a failure as a magician."

Then all at once, Rodney had an idea. He made a big sign that said RODNEY'S RESTAURANT. Then he went into the kitchen and started to cook.

Well, it wasn't long before people started coming to Rodney's Restaurant. Sparky Smith came too. And he said something that made Rodney beam with joy.

Sparky had finished a big sandwich, and said, "Wow! This sandwich is good! You're not just a great cook, Rodney. No, sir. You're a magician in the kitchen."

How do you think Rodney felt when people stopped asking him to do magic tricks? Rodney showed his feelings by something he said and did. He said he was a flop and began to cry. His actions and words showed that Rodney was very unhappy.

290

RODNEY'S RESTAURANT

How did Rodney feel when Sparky said Rodney was a great cook? How did Rodney show his feelings?

What kind of person do you think Rodney is? Did he give up when things didn't go his way? What did Rodney do that shows he doesn't give up easily? He opened a restaurant in order to use his special talent.

Practice

Think about the things Sparky Smith said and did in the story to answer the following questions.

1. How did Sparky feel about Rodney's magic in the beginning of the story? What did Sparky say that helps you understand his feelings?
2. How did Sparky feel about the food at Rodney's Restaurant? How do you know?

Look at what the character says and does in the next selection, "Kevin Cloud, Chippewa Boy in the City," to help you understand his feelings and the kind of person he is.

Kevin Cloud,
Chippewa Boy in the City

by Carol Ann Bales

My name is Kevin Wayne Cloud.

I was born on Thanksgiving Day in Cook County Hospital in Chicago. I'm a Native American. My family belongs to the Chippewas. We live in the city. I'm ten years old.

I've got two older sisters, Sheila and Brenda, and a little brother, Mark. Then there's Dino, our dog, and Joey, our cat. And, of course, there's Mama. My uncle Obe lives with us too, and Grandma.

We got Dino from a neighbor. He was funny looking, but we loved him anyway. Sometimes my friends and I play football with Dino. Mostly he chases us and we tackle him. But we let him make a touchdown every once in a while so he won't feel bad.

My friends and I also like to play baseball. Sometimes Grandma plays with us. Once she slid into home plate. That was funny.

Grandma babysits with Mark and my two little cousins while Mama and my aunt are at work. Mama works at the Montrose Urban Progress Center. They're supposed to help people find jobs. She keeps records. She says it's hard work.

Every day, when Mama leaves for work, I leave for school. The first thing I do when I get home from school is get out my bike. I like to ride my bike more than anything else. I ride a lot with my cousin Myron. Myron's nine. He lives down the street. I ride with Andy too. He lives upstairs. But I'd rather go bike riding with Myron. Andy doesn't have a lock and chain on his bicycle. Myron does.

When I ride with Myron, we stop and lock our bikes together. Myron pins the key to his shirt so he won't lose it. When Myron isn't around, I bring my bike inside. Otherwise it might get stolen. I bring it in when my legs get tired.

Myron and I go everywhere. Mama says, "That Kevin, he really gets around. He knows more people than I do."

Sometimes we go down to Lincoln Park Zoo and to the North Avenue Beach. Once we went almost all the way downtown. Myron didn't know his way home, but I did.

Mama and Grandma and the rest of my family used to live in Cass Lake, Minnesota, on Leech Lake Reservation. Mama says there were no jobs there and no places to go. She came to Chicago before I was born.

Grandma says the Chippewa have lived on Leech Lake for a long, long time. There's an old story, a legend, about how the Chippewa came to live in Minnesota. My grandfather used to tell it.

The Great Spirit sent a crane to fly across the sky and find a place for the Chippewa to live. As he flew over one lake, Lake Superior, he gave out a loud cry. He was answered by a loon. A loon is a bird. So the crane knew that it was a good place to live.

My grandfather belonged to the Loon clan, and so Mama is a member of the Loon clan too. A clan is like a big family.

I don't have a real Chippewa name, but my sister Brenda does. She was born in Cass Lake. They had a naming ceremony for her up there. Her Chippewa name is something like *C-Kwa-Duke*. But she doesn't ever use it. She says nobody could spell it or say it.

Grandma speaks Chippewa. Mama does too. So do all my aunts and uncles. I understand a few words. Grandma tries to teach us.

Grandma is always going to powwows. I go once in a while. When we went to a powwow last summer, Grandma wore a Chippewa dress that she made. She has five Indian dresses. Three are Chippewa with beadwork. The other two have ribbons. A Winnebago lady made them.

I wore some moccasins from Cass Lake and danced the rabbit dance.

Grandma helped cook and serve. The food we had was fry bread and hominy. But I liked the fried chicken best. That's one of my favorite foods. Grandma gave me a nice piece.

It was cold that night, and people started a big fire that we could sit around to keep warm. They danced for a long time. Grandma said it was a real good powwow that night.

Last summer we went up to the reservation in Minnesota to harvest wild rice and to visit Aunt Rose. She's Mama's cousin. It was a long way. I kept asking how much farther it was.

I was little when I was in Minnesota last time, and I didn't remember much. We don't go up very often. It's too far. Grandma has gone up more times. She pointed out things on the way. Once she pointed out the Chippewa River.

Finally we got to Aunt Rose's house. She lives in the town of Cass Lake. I was happy. Soon I would get a chance to go ricing.

Aunt Rose goes ricing on a lake. There are many birch trees along the path where she launches her boat. Grandma says the place was an old campsite. She says not everybody knew about it. She remembers when they used to camp there.

The old Chippewa used the bark from the white birch trees to make canoes, to cover their wig-wams, and for rice trays and sugar baskets. They knew how to strip the bark from the trees with-out killing them. Grandma says she used to watch my great-grandfather making canoes. She says everybody who knew how to make them is probably dead, and besides, it's hard to get the wood. That's why they don't make them now.

It rained the first day of ricing. But Aunt Rose said that wouldn't make any difference. Everybody got up early. We saw many cars with boats on top.

Aunt Rose doesn't have her own boat. She rented one from a man. She had to sell her rice to him. She also bought a license and a pair of knockers. Knockers are long wooden sticks. They are used to knock the rice into the boat.

Aunt Rose dropped some tobacco in the water before she started ricing. Mama says that's the old way of giving thanks for the rice.

When we were done ricing, we went back to Aunt Rose's house. I played with my cousins for a while. That was fun. Before we left for home, Mama bought some wild rice at the store. We usually have white rice at home. Mama says the wild rice you buy in Chicago doesn't taste right, and it costs too much money.

When we got back home, we were all tired. I started pestering Mama to let me have a birthday party. My tenth birthday was coming up. She said she'd think about it. My sister Brenda said, "Why don't you let him have a party?" When she said that I felt glad she was my sister.

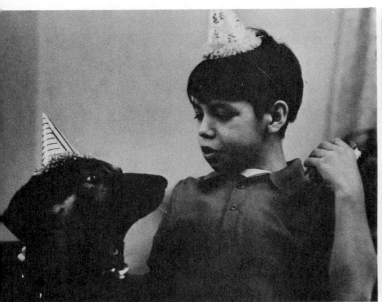

Myron, Bryant, and Little Kevin came to my
birthday party. Little Kevin is shorter than I
am. That's why they call him Little Kevin.

At my party we ate lots of delicious things.
Grandma made some hominy. I always help her cut
off the corn for the hominy. She made a lot, but
it didn't last very long. My aunts all came over
to get some. They like Grandma's hominy.

I got a lot of presents. I got some money,
long underwear from Mama, and a rodeo set. I
also got some little cars, but my brother Mark
broke them. Sometimes I think you can't keep anything around here.

After I opened my presents, we went outside.
It was my first birthday party. I'll probably
remember it a long time.

Comprehension Check

1. What is Kevin Cloud's favorite thing to do?
2. From the way Kevin described the powwow, do you think he enjoyed it? Why or why not?
3. Do you think Kevin likes learning about the history and customs of his family? Why or why not?
4. Would you find it interesting to learn about the history and customs of your family? Why or why not?

Skill Check

Think about the things Kevin Cloud said and did in the story to answer the following questions.

1. How do you think Kevin feels about being a Chippewa? What does he say or do that tells you how he feels?
2. How do you think Kevin feels about his dog, Dino? What does he say and do that tells you how he feels?
3. How does Kevin feel about his grandma? What does he say and do that tells you how he feels?
4. How does Kevin feel about going ricing? What does he say or do that tells you how he feels?
5. Kevin's sister says, "Why don't you let him have a party?" How does this make Kevin feel about her? What does he say that tells you how he feels?

How Old Is Old?

by Leonore Klein

Who is old? Are you old? Or are you young? What is really old? Is sixty old? Is eight old? It's hard to say.

In the garden where Michael plays in the spring lives a family of mayflies. They are pretty flies. They have delicate wings and threadlike tails.

Mayflies are born in the late springtime or early summer. They eat no food and they take nothing to drink. They live for a day or, at most, three days.

A mayfly is old when it is *three days old*!

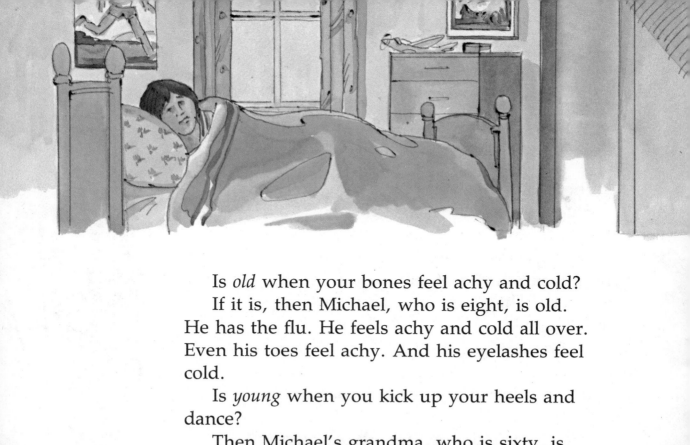

Is *old* when your bones feel achy and cold?

If it is, then Michael, who is eight, is old.
He has the flu. He feels achy and cold all over.
Even his toes feel achy. And his eyelashes feel
cold.

Is *young* when you kick up your heels and
dance?

Then Michael's grandma, who is sixty, is
young. Watch her whirl around as she dances.

"You're as young as you feel," says Grandma.
"And I feel young. I feel like dancing."

Down in the cellar of Michael's house lives a small gray mouse. If Michael's mother knew he lived there, she would set a trap and try to catch him. But she doesn't.

This mouse is four years old, just the same age as Michael's younger sister, Emily. But this mouse is an old mouse. He has grandchildren and great-grandchildren, and even great-great-great-great-grandchildren.

Mice don't live to be older than *four years.*

Sometimes a squirrel comes to play in the oak tree in Michael's garden. This squirrel likes to eat acorns when they fall from the tree.

Michael and Emily don't know how old this squirrel is. They call him "Quickie," because he scampers away from them so quickly.

Michael would be surprised to know that he and this squirrel have the same birth date. They were both born eight years, four days, and six hours ago. Michael is a young boy. But Quickie is an old, old squirrel.

How old is old for a furry gray squirrel? *Eight years* is old!

Emily and Michael have a dog. Arnold Appleby, who lives next door, has a cat. Emily and Michael's dog and Arnold Appleby's cat never fight. That is because Arnold's cat is too old and too lazy to hiss or spit at a dog. She is nearly fifteen years old.

Emily and Michael's dog is one year old. He is still a puppy. He barks and barks at Arnold's cat. But Arnold's cat just sits still and looks at him.

Cats and dogs are old cats and dogs when they are about *fifteen years old*—almost Arnold Appleby's age.

Michael and Emily don't see horses very often. But they like to look at pictures of horses in newspapers. They especially like to look at pictures of Scarlet. Scarlet is a famous race-horse, with a proud head and high-stepping feet. Scarlet is three years old. A three-year-old is a grown-up horse.

Sometimes there are pictures of Scarlet's grandfather in the papers too. Scarlet's grand-father was once the greatest racehorse in the whole world. Now all he does is chew on oats and rest in a field. He's twenty-eight years old.

Horses come to the end of their lives when they are less than *thirty years old*. Michael's father, who is thirty years old, sometimes wishes all he had to do was rest in a field.

310

When Emily and Michael go to the zoo, they like to look at the two hippopotamuses. They can't tell the old hippopotamus from the young hippopotamus, because the old hippopotamus and the young hippopotamus both look the same—very fat and very tough-skinned.

The fact of the matter is, a hippopotamus is an old hippopotamus when it's *forty years old*.

A swan is an old swan when it is *forty-five years old*. Emily and Michael's grandma once had a swan living on the pond on her farm. It flew away one year and never came back.

Elephants live even longer than swans. Parrots live even longer than elephants. And people live even longer than parrots.

An elephant is old at *fifty*. A parrot is old at *sixty-five*. A person is old at *eighty*.

Emily and Michael's great-grandma, who is eighty, might be considered old. But when she paints or goes fishing, Emily and Michael think of her as young.

Once Emily and Michael went to the aquarium. There they saw the oldest animal of all. It was a giant tortoise and it was *150 years old*!

The earth we live on is billions of years old.

Michael isn't billions of years old. Michael is eight. But Michael can read and write, ride a two-wheeler bike, and play the piano. That's why his sister Emily, who is only four, thinks he is old. She can't read or write or ride a two-wheeler bike. She can't play the piano either.

Michael doesn't think he is old, but he'd like to be. He'd like to be as old as Arnold Appleby.

Arnold Appleby goes to high school. He plays the drums in the high-school band and delivers papers on a motorbike. Arnold Appleby is sixteen.

Arnold Appleby doesn't think he is old. He thinks Michael's parents are old. Michael's father is thirty. Michael's mother is thirty too. Michael's father and mother can stay up until one o'clock in the morning if they want to. And they both have important jobs in the city.

Michael's father doesn't think he and Michael's mother are old. He thinks his *own* mother is old. His mother is Michael's grandma, and she is sixty. Her hair is getting white.

She doesn't think she is old. But she has a friend who is eighty years old. "That's really old," says Michael's grandma.

"You're as old as you feel, and I feel young," says Michael's grandma's friend. "I feel like dancing."

314

As Michael's grandma's friend says, "You are as old as you feel."

How old are you? Do you feel old? Or do you feel young?

Michael drew up a graph showing what is old for some of the animals in the story you just read. Find your age on this graph. Which animals are young at your age? Which animals are old at your age? Do you have a pet at home or in the classroom? Where would it be on this graph?

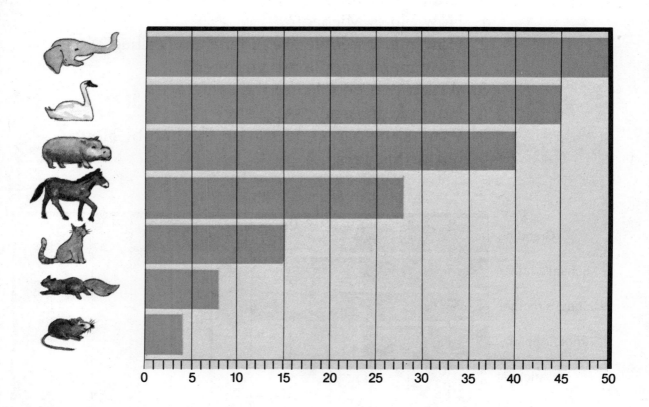

Comprehension Check
1. How old is old for a parrot?
2. What does Grandma's friend mean when she says, "You're as old as you feel."
3. Do you think it's true that people are as old as they feel? Why or why not?
4. If you could be one of the animals in this story, which one would you choose to be? Tell why.

Skill Check
Look at the graph below. Then answer the questions that follow.
1. How old is Michael?
2. How many people are older than Michael? How many people are younger?
3. Which two people are the same age?
4. How old is Arnold Appleby?
5. Who is the oldest person on the graph? How old is this person?

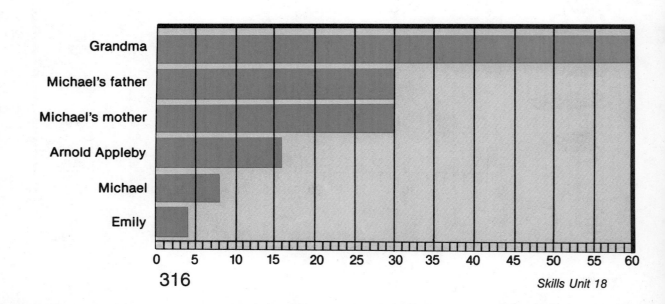

Freckle Juice

by Judy Blume

Literary Unit

Gold Medal
Selection

Andrew Marcus wanted freckles. Nicky Lane
had freckles. He had about a million of them. They
covered his face, his ears, and the back of his
neck. Andrew didn't have any freckles. If he had
freckles like Nicky, his mother would never know
if his neck was dirty. So he wouldn't have to
wash. And then he'd never be late for school.

Andrew had plenty of time to look at Nicky's
freckles. He sat right behind him in class. Once
he even tried to count them. But when he got to
eighty-six, Miss Kelly called, "Andrew . . . are
you paying attention?"

Later that day, when the bell rang, Andrew poked Nicky Lane.

"What do you want?" Nicky asked, turning around.

"I was wondering about your freckles," Andrew said.

"Oh, yeah? What about them?"

Andrew felt pretty stupid. "Well, how did you get them?"

"What do you mean *how*? You get born with them. That's how!"

Andrew thought that's what Nicky would say. Some help *he* was.

"Psst . . ." a girl named Sharon whispered to Andrew. "I know how to get them."

"How to get what?" Andrew asked.

"Freckles," Sharon said.

"Who asked *you*?" Andrew wanted to know.

Literary Unit

"I heard you ask Nicky about his. Do you want to know how to get them?" Sharon asked.

"Maybe," Andrew told her.

"It'll cost you fifty cents. I have a secret recipe for freckle juice," Sharon whispered.

"A secret recipe? You don't even have freckles," Andrew said.

"Look close," Sharon said. "I've got six on my nose."

"Big deal! A lot of good six will do."

"You can get as many as you want," Sharon told Andrew. "Six was enough for me. It all depends on how much freckle juice you drink."

Andrew didn't believe Sharon for a minute; not one minute! There was no such thing as freckle juice. Andrew had never heard of it before!

That night Andrew had trouble sleeping. He kept thinking about freckle juice. Maybe the reason no one in his family had freckles was because no one knew the secret recipe. If they never even heard of freckle juice, then how could they have freckles? It figured!

Andrew didn't like the idea of paying Sharon for anything. And fifty cents was a lot of money. But he decided that if Sharon's recipe didn't work he'd ask for his money back. It was easy.

The next morning Andrew turned the combination of his safe-bank to just the right numbers. He took out five dimes. He wrapped them in a tissue and stuffed the whole thing in his pocket.

320

Andrew raced to school. He could hardly wait to see the secret recipe. First he'd look at it, and if it didn't seem any good, he just wouldn't pay.

Sharon was already at her desk when Andrew arrived. He went right over to her.

"Did you bring it?" he asked.

"Bring what?" Sharon opened her eyes real wide.

"You know what! The secret recipe for freckle juice."

"Oh, that! I have it—right here." Sharon patted her pocket.

"Well, let's see it," said Andrew.

"Do you have fifty cents?" Sharon asked.

Andrew shook his head. "Oh, no! First I want to see it."

"Sorry, Andrew. A deal's a deal!" Sharon opened a book and pretended to read.

Andrew went to his seat. Then he took the tissue with the five dimes out of his pocket. He held it near the floor and aimed it toward Sharon.

Sharon sat in the next row. She stuck out her foot and stepped on the tissue. Then she bent down and picked it up. Miss Kelly didn't notice.

Sharon counted the five dimes. Then she took a piece of folded-up white paper out of her pocket and threw it to Andrew. It landed in the middle of the aisle. Andrew leaned way over to pick it up. But he lost his balance and fell off his chair. Everybody laughed, except Andrew and Miss Kelly.

Miss Kelly sighed. "Oh, Andrew! What are you up to now? Bring me that note, please."

Literary Unit

Andrew picked up the secret recipe. He didn't even have a chance to see it. It wasn't fair. It cost him fifty cents for nothing. He handed it to Miss Kelly. She read it. Then she looked up at him. "Andrew, you may have this back at three o'clock." She put it in her desk. "I don't want this to happen again. Do you understand?"

"Yes, Miss Kelly," Andrew mumbled.

At three o'clock, when the second bell finally rang, Andrew went up to Miss Kelly.

"Here's your note, Andrew," she said. "I have the feeling it's important to you. But from now on you must pay attention in class."

Andrew took the recipe from Miss Kelly. "After tomorrow I won't have any trouble paying attention," he promised. "Just you wait, Miss Kelly. I won't have any trouble at all."

Andrew ran all the way home. The secret recipe for freckle juice was folded carefully in the bottom of Andrew's shoe. He was going to put it inside his sock, but he was afraid if his foot got sweaty the ink might blur and he wouldn't be able to read it. Even if it was windy nothing could happen to it there. He made up his mind not to read it until he got home. He didn't want to waste any time getting there. And he wasn't the world's fastest reader anyway, even though he'd gotten better since last fall. Still, there might be some hard words that would take a while to figure out.

Andrew dashed to his house, unlocked the front door, and took off his shoe as soon as he was inside. He pulled out the secret recipe and sat down on the floor to read it. It said:

SHARON'S SECRET RECIPE FOR FRECKLE JUICE
One glass makes an average amount of freckles. To get like Nicky Lane drink two glasses. Mix up all these things together stir well and drink fast. Grape juice, vinegar, mustard, mayonnaise, juice from one lemon, pepper and salt, olive oil and a speck of onion.
P.S. The faster you drink it the faster you get FRECKLES.

Andrew read the list twice. It didn't sound like much of a secret recipe. His mother used those things every day. Of course, she didn't use them all together. Maybe that was the secret part. Well, he'd paid fifty cents. He might as well find out.

He chose a big blue glass. He'd start with just one glassful and then drink another if he wanted more freckles. No point in overdoing it the first time. That's what his mother always said.

He put all the ingredients into the glass. It smelled awful! JUST PLAIN AWFUL! He'd have to hold his nose while he drank it. It said to drink it very fast! That old Sharon! She probably thought he wouldn't be able to drink it. Well, he'd show her. He'd drink it all right.

Andrew held his nose, tilted his head back, and gulped down Sharon's secret recipe for freckle juice. Then he crept into his mother's bedroom. He didn't feel well enough to walk. He sat on the floor in front of the full-length mirror. He waited for something to happen.

Pretty soon something happened, all right. Andrew turned greenish and felt very sick. His stomach hurt. At four o'clock Mrs. Marcus came home. She walked into her bedroom.

"Andrew Marcus, you're green! *Absolutely green!*" she said. "I've just seen that mess in the kitchen. Did you or did you not make something and eat it?"

Oh-oh! He forgot to clean up. Now she knew. Well, he didn't care. His stomach was killing him.

Andrew closed his eyes.

"Now, young man . . . you are going to bed!" said his mother.

Andrew thought that was the best idea he'd heard in a long time. Mrs. Marcus gave him two spoonfuls of pink stuff that tasted like peppermint. Then she tucked him into bed.

The next day Andrew stayed home from school. He only looked in the mirror once—no freckles!

The following day his mother woke him up and sang, "Time for school. Rise and shine!"

"I'm not going to school today," Andrew said. "I'm never going to school again." He hid his head under his pillow. He wasn't going to let Sharon see him without freckles. She wasn't going to get the chance to laugh at him. No sir!

Big Blue

Blue Whale by Andrew

"Andrew," said his mother. "I want to see you up and dressed before I count to fifteen or you're going to take three baths a day, every day for the next ten years!"

Andrew got dressed. But still he couldn't let Sharon get away with it. He had to do something. He opened his desk drawer and looked for a brown marker. All he could find was a blue one. He put the marker into his lunch box and headed for school. He stopped two blocks before he got there. Then he took out the marker and decorated his whole face and neck with blue dots. Maybe they didn't look like Nicky Lane's freckles, but they sure looked like something!

Andrew waited until the second bell rang. Then he hurried to his class and sat down. He heard a lot of whispering, but he didn't look around.

Miss Kelly snapped her fingers. "Let's settle down, children. Stop chattering." Everybody giggled. "What's so funny? Just what is so funny? Lisa, can you tell me the joke?"

Lisa stood up. "It's Andrew, Miss Kelly. Just look at Andrew Marcus."

Miss Kelly looked at Andrew. "Goodness," she said. "What have you done to yourself?"

"I grew freckles, Miss Kelly. That's what!" Andrew knew his blue dots looked silly but he didn't care. He turned toward Sharon and stuck out his tongue. Sharon made a frog face at him.

Miss Kelly took a deep breath. "I see," she said. "Well, let's get on with our morning work."

At recess, Nicky Lane turned around and said, "Whoever heard of blue freckles?"

Andrew didn't answer him. He sat in class all day with his blue freckles. Then at two o'clock Miss Kelly called him to her desk.

"Andrew," Miss Kelly said. "How would you like to use my secret formula for removing freckles?" Her voice was low, but not so low that the class couldn't hear.

"For free?" Andrew asked.

"Oh, yes," Miss Kelly said. "For free."

Andrew scratched his head and thought it over.

Miss Kelly took a small package out of her desk. She handed it to Andrew. "Now, don't open this until you get to the Boys' Room. Remember, it's a *secret formula*. OK?"

"OK," Andrew said.

Andrew wanted to run to the Boys' Room, but he knew the rules. No running in the halls. So he walked as fast as he could. He couldn't wait to see what was in the package. Could there really be such a thing as freckle remover?

As soon as he was inside the Boys' Room he unwrapped the package. There was a note. Andrew read it. It said:

> TURN ON WATER. WET MAGIC FRECKLE
> REMOVER AND RUB INTO FACE. RINSE.
> IF MAGIC FRECKLE REMOVER DOES NOT
> WORK FIRST TIME . . . TRY AGAIN.
> THREE TIMES SHOULD DO THE JOB.
>
> MISS KELLY

Ha! Miss Kelly knew. She knew all the time. She knew his freckles weren't really freckles. But she didn't tell.

Andrew followed Miss Kelly's directions. The magic freckle remover smelled like lemons. Andrew had to use it four times to get his freckles off. Then he wrapped it up and walked back to his classroom.

Miss Kelly smiled. "Well, Andrew. I see it worked."

"Yes, Miss Kelly. It sure did," said Andrew.

"You look fine now, Andrew. You know, I think you're a very handsome boy without freckles!"

"You *do*?" said Andrew.

"Yes, I do."

"Miss Kelly . . . Miss Kelly!" Nicky Lane called out, raising his hand and waving it around.

"What is it, Nicky?" Miss Kelly asked.

"Could I use your magic freckle remover?" Nicky asked. "Could I, Miss Kelly? I hate my freckles. I hate every single one of them!"

Andrew couldn't believe it. How could Nicky hate his freckles? They were so neat!

"Nicky," Miss Kelly said. "Andrew didn't look good with freckles. But you look wonderful! I'd hate to see you without them. They're part of you. So I'm going to put away this magic formula. I hope I never have to use it again."

Well, Andrew thought. She'd never have to use it on *him*. He was *through* with freckles.

When the class lined up to go home, Andrew heard Sharon whisper to Nicky, "I know how to get rid of them."

"Get rid of what?" Nicky asked.

"Your freckles," she said.

"You do?" he exclaimed.

"Sure. The secret recipe for removing freckles has been in my family for years. That's how come none of us have any. I'll sell it to you for fifty cents!"

Then Sharon walked up alongside Andrew. Before Andrew could say a word, Sharon made a super-duper frog face just for him!

334

Glossary

Full Pronunciation Key

The pronunciation of each word is shown just after the word, in this way:
ab bre vi ate (ə brē′vē āt).

The letters and signs used are pronounced as the words below.

The mark ′ is placed after a syllable with primary or heavy accent, as in the example above.

The mark ′ after a syllable shows a secondary or lighter accent, as in **ab bre vi ation** (ə brē′vē ā′shən).

a	hat, cap	**j**	jam, enjoy	**u**	cup, butter
ā	age, face	**k**	kind, seek	**u̇**	full, put
ä	father, far	**l**	land, coal	**ü**	rule, move
		m	me, am		
b	bad, rob	**n**	no, in	**v**	very, save
ch	child, much	**ng**	long, bring	**w**	will, woman
d	did, red			**y**	young, yet
		o	hot, rock	**z**	zero, breeze
e	let, best	**ō**	open, go	**zh**	measure, seizure
ē	equal, be	**ô**	order, all		
ėr	term, learn	**oi**	oil, voice		
		ou	house, out	**ə**	represents:
f	fat, if				a in about
g	go, bag	**p**	paper, cup		e in taken
h	he, how	**r**	run, try		i in pencil
		s	say, yes		o in lemon
i	it, pin	**sh**	she, rush		u in circus
ī	ice, five	**t**	tell, it		
		th	thin, both		
		ŦH	then, smooth		

A a

ab sorb (ab sôrb′), **1** take in and hold: *Rugs absorb sounds and make a house quieter.* **2** take up all the attention of; interest very much: *She was absorbed in reading that book. verb.*

a chieve (ə chēv′), **1** reach by one's own efforts: *She achieved fame as a swimmer.* **2** do; carry out: *Did you achieve all that you expected to today? verb,* **a chieved, a chiev ing.**

ach y (āk′ē), feeling discomfort; slight pain: *Sally's body felt achy. adjective.*

a corn (ā′kôrn), the nut of an oak tree. *noun.*

aer o nau tics (er′ə nô′tiks *or* ar′ə nô′tiks), science or art having to do with the design, building, and operation of aircraft. *noun.*

aisle (īl), **1** passage between rows of seats in a hall, theater, or school. **2** any long, narrow passage. *noun.*

a lu mi num (ə lü′mə nəm), a very light, silver-white metal that does not rust easily. *noun.*

anx ious (angk′shəs), **1** worried because of thoughts or fears of what may happen: *Lee felt anxious about his spelling test.* **2** wishing very much; eager: *They were anxious to start their trip. adjective;* **anx ious ly,** *adverb.*

ap pen di ci tis (ə pen′də sī′tis), soreness and swelling of a part of the body called the appendix. *noun.*

a quar i um (ə kwer′ē əm), **1** building used for showing collections of living fish, water animals, and water plants. **2** tank or glass bowl in which living fish, other water animals, and water plants are kept. *noun.*

as tro phys i cist (as′trō fiz′ə sist), a scientist who studies the planets and stars. *noun.*

av er age (av′ər ij), **1** amount found by dividing the sum of a few numbers by how many numbers there are: *The average of 3 and 5 and 10 is 6 (because 3 + 5 + 10 = 18 and 18 ÷ 3 = 6).* **2** usual sort or amount: *The amount of rain this year has been below average.* **3** usual; ordinary: *The average person likes TV.* **1,2** *noun,* **3** *adjective.*

av o ca do (av′ə kä′dō), the fruit of a tree that grows in warm areas. Avocados are shaped like pears and have a dark-green skin and a very large seed. *noun, plural* **av o ca dos.**

ax (aks), tool with a flat, sharp blade attached to a handle, used for chopping, splitting, and shaping wood. See picture. *noun, plural* **ax es.**

ax

B b

bal last (bal′əst), something heavy carried in a ship to steady it. *noun.*

bal let (bal′ā), a dance by a group on a stage. A ballet usually tells a story through the movements of the dancing and the music. *noun.*

ban is ter (ban′ə stər), railing you hold onto when you go down the stairs. *noun.*

bank (bangk), **1** a long pile or heap: *a bank of snow.* **2** pile up; heap up: *Tractors banked the snow by the roadside.* **3** ground bordering a river or lake; shore. **1,3** *noun,* **2** *verb.*

base (bās), **1** gotten from: *Jamie's story was based on fact.* **2** the part on which anything stands or rests; bottom: *The big machine has a wide steel base.* **1** *verb,* **based, bas ing; 2** *noun.*

bead work (bēd′werk′), a thing, usually for decoration, made with or of beads. *noun.*

bear a ble (ber′ə bəl) able to put up with: *The noise was bearable. adverb.*

bil low (bil′ō), **1** rise or roll in big waves: *Waves billowed toward the shore.* **2** a great swelling wave. **3** swell out; bulge: *Sheets on a line billow in the wind.* **1,3** *verb,* **2** *noun.*

bi noc u lars (bə nok′yə lərz), something that you look through that makes things far away look closer. *noun plural.*

birch (bėrch), **1** a slender, strong tree with a smooth bark that peels off in thin layers. See picture. **2** its hard wood; often used in making furniture. *noun, plural* **birch es** *for 1.*

birch tree

blaze (blāz), **1** burn with a bright flame: *A fire was blazing in the fireplace.* **2** glare; glow of brightness: *the blaze of the noon sun.* 1 *verb,* **blazed, blaz ing;** 2 *noun, plural* **blaz es.**

blos som (blos′əm), **1** flower, especially of a plant that produces fruit: *apple blossoms.* **2** condition or time of flowering: *pear trees in blossom. noun.*

blur (blėr), **1** smear; smudge: *I blurred my painting by touching it before the paint was dry.* **2** make less clear in form or outline: *Mist blurred the hills.* **3** dim: *Tears blurred my eyes.* **4** thing seen dimly: *Without my glasses on, your face is just a blur.* 1,2,3 *verb,* **blurred, blur ring;** 4 *noun.*

bolt (bōlt), **1** a streak of lightning. **2** a sliding fastening for a door or gate. **3** dash off; run away. 1,2 *noun,* 3 *verb.*

bond (bond), **1** anything that ties, binds, or unites: *There is a bond of love between sisters.* **2** bonds, chains: *the bonds of slavery. noun.*

brine (brīn), very salty water. Some pickles are kept in brine. *noun.*

bud (bud), **1** a small growth on a plant that will grow into a flower, leaf, or branch: *Buds on the trees are a sign of spring.* **2** a partly opened flower or leaf. **3** put forth buds. 1,2 *noun,* 3 *verb,* **bud ded, bud ding.**

a hat	**i** it	**oi** oil	**ch** child	a in about
ā age	**ī** ice	**ou** out	**ng** long	e in taken
ä far	**o** hot	**u** cup	**sh** she	ə = { i in pencil
e let	**ō** open	**ù** put	**th** thin	o in lemon
ē equal	**ô** order	**ü** rule	**ŦH** then	u in circus
ėr term			**zh** measure	

burst (bėrst), **1** go, come, or do by force or suddenly: *Don't burst into the room without knocking.* **2** open or be opened suddenly: *The trees burst into bloom.* **3** fly apart suddenly with force; explode: *If you stick a pin into a balloon, it will burst.* **4** bursting; outbreak: *There was a burst of laughter when the clown fell.* 1,2,3 *verb,* **burst, burst ing;** 4 *noun.*

C c

Can a da (Kan′ə də), country in North America, on the northern border of the United States. *noun.*

ca noe (kə nü′), **1** a light boat pointed at both ends and moved with a paddle. See picture. **2** paddle a canoe; go in a canoe. 1 *noun,* 2 *verb,* **ca noed, ca noe ing.**

paddling a canoe

car a van (kar′ə van), any long line of cars, carts, or wagons with people traveling together from place to place. *noun.*

car ou sel (kar′ə sel′), a merry-go-round. *noun.*

cart (kärt), **1** carrying something: *Cart away this garbage.* **2** a strong wagon with two wheels used in farming and for carrying heavy loads. **3** a light wagon used to deliver goods. **4** a small metal wagon moved by hand: *a grocery cart.* **1** *verb,* **2,3,4** *noun.*

cha me le on (kə mē′lē ən), a small lizard that can change the color of its skin to blend with the surroundings. See picture. *noun.*

chameleon

chance (chans), **1** take the risk of: *Don't chance driving in this storm.* **2** a favorable time: *Now is your chance to earn some money.* **3** possibility: *There is a good chance that you will win this race.* **4** happen: *I chanced to meet an old friend today.* **5** risk: *You will be taking a chance if you try to swim that lake.* **1,4** *verb,* **chanced, chanc ing;** **2,3,5** *noun.*

chan de lier (shan′də lir′), something you hang from the ceiling for light. It usually has branches to which bulbs are attached. *noun.*

Chi ca go (shə kä′gō), a city in the midwestern state of Illinois. *noun.*

chi na (chī′nə), **1** a fine white clay baked in a special way. It was first used in China. Dishes and other things are made of china. *noun.*

Chip pe wa (chip′ə wa), the English word for a group of Native Americans whose home is in North America near the Great Lakes. The Native American name for this group is Ojibwa. *noun,* *plural* **Chip pe was.**

chute (shüt), a steep slide: *The mail chute carries mail to a lower level. noun.*

cli mate (klī′mit), **1** the kind of weather a place has. Climate includes conditions of heat and cold, moisture and dryness, clearness and cloudiness, wind and calm. **2** a region with certain weather conditions: *We went to a warmer climate on our winter vacation. noun.*

col lage (kəl äzh′), picture made by pasting such things as parts of newspapers, string, and colored paper on another paper or cardboard. See picture. *noun.* (*Collage* comes from a French word meaning "pasting" or "gluing.")

collage

col umn (kol′əm), **1** anything that is tall and upright: *A column of smoke rose from the fire.* **2** something slim and upright, usually made of stone, wood, or metal, and used to hold up part of a building. **3** a narrow division of a page reading from top to bottom, kept separate by lines or blank spaces. *noun.*

com bi na tion (kom′bə nā′shən), **1** group or set of numbers or letters used to open a lock or safe. **2** one whole thing made by joining together two or more different things: *The color purple is a combination of red and blue. noun.*

com pound (kom′pound) **1** a mixture: *Many medicines are compounds.* **2** having more than one part: *"Anymore" is a compound word because it has two words in it, "any" and "more." noun.*

con demn (kən dem′), **1** call something not safe for use: *The bridge was condemned because it is no longer safe.* **2** express feelings or thoughts against: *We condemn cruelty to animals. verb.*

con ser va tion ist (kon′sər vā′shən ist), person who is interested in protecting things from being used up or lost; person whose job it is to protect things like animals, trees, water, etc., from being wasted or used up. *noun.*

con stant (kon′stənt), **1** never stopping: *Three days of constant rain made the field muddy.* **2** continually happening: *A clock makes a constant ticking sound.* **3** always the same; not changing. **4** faithful; loyal: *A constant friend helps you when you need help. adjective.*

con sump tion (kən sump′shən), act of eating; using up. *noun.*

con tam i nate (kən tam′ə nāt), make something dirty or unhealthy by touching it: *The water was contaminated by garbage. verb,* **con tam i nat ed, con tam i nat ing.**

con ven ient (kən vē′nyənt), within easy reach; handy; easily done; easy to use: *Let's meet at a convenient place. adjective.*

con vey or or **con vey er** (kən vā′ər), **1** something that carries things from one place to another: *The conveyor belt carries the boxes from floor to floor.* **2** a person who carries things from one place to another. *noun.*

cor net (kôr net′), a musical instrument like a trumpet, usually of brass. See picture. *noun.*

cornet

cot ton wood (kot′n wùd′), **1** a kind of tree with soft white balls on its seeds that look like cotton. **2** soft wood of this tree. *noun.*

coy o te (kī ō′tē *or* kī′ōt), a small wolflike animal living in the western part of North America. *noun, plural* **coy o tes** *or* **coy o te.**

crane (krān), **1** machine with a long swinging arm for lifting heavy things. **2** a large wading bird with long legs, neck, and bill. **3** stretch in order to see better. **1,2** *noun,* **3** *verb,* **craned, cran ing.**

a hat	i it	oi oil	ch child	(a in about
ā age	ī ice	ou out	ng long	e in taken
ä far	o hot	u cup	sh she	ə = ⟨ i in pencil
e let	ō open	ù put	th thin	o in lemon
ē equal	ô order	ü rule	ŦH then	u in circus
ėr term			zh measure	

cre a tive (krē ā′tiv), having the ability to come up with something new; inventive: *creative artists. adjective.*

crim son (krim′zən), **1** deep red. **2** turn deep red in color. **1** *adjective,* **2** *verb.*

cruise (krüz), **1** sail about from place to place: *We cruised to Bermuda on our vacation.* **2** voyage for pleasure with no special destination in view: *We went for a cruise on the Great Lakes.* **1** *verb,* **cruised, cruis ing; 2** *noun.*

crust (krust), **1** the solid outside part of the earth. See picture. **2** the hard outside part of bread. **3** dough rolled out thin and baked for pies. **4** cover with a crust; form into a crust; become covered with a crust. **1,2,3** *noun,* **4** *verb.*

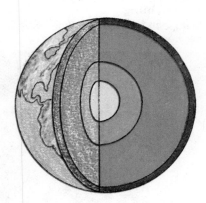

earth's **crust** (definition 1)

cush ion (kùsh′ən), **1** soften or ease: *Nothing could cushion us from the ride on the bumpy road.* **2** soft pillow or pad used to sit or lie on. **1** *verb,* **2** *noun.*

339

D d

dare dev il (dar/dev/əl), a person who does dangerous things. *noun.*

de sign (də zīn/), **1** plan out; arrange form and color of: *We designed a tree house.* **2** arrangement of details, form, and color in painting, weaving, or building. **3** a drawing, plan, or sketch made to serve as a pattern from which to work: *The design showed how to build the machine.* 1 *verb,* 2,3 *noun.*

de sire (di zīr/), **1** wish: *My desire is to travel.* **2** wish earnestly for. **3** ask for: *The principal desires your presence in her office.* **4** thing wished for: *His greatest desire was for a dog.* 1,4 *noun,* 2,3 *verb,* **de sired, de sir ing.**

dic tate (dik/tāt), **1** say or read (something) aloud for another person to write down: *The teacher dictated a list of words to the students.* **2** make others do what one says: *Big countries sometimes dictate to little ones. verb,* **dic tat ed, dic tat ing.**

dis a ble (dis ā/bəl), make unable; cripple: *A sprained wrist disabled the tennis player. verb,* **dis a bled, dis a bling.**

down[1] (doun), soft feathers: *the down of a bird.* See picture. *noun.*

down-feathered
baby chick
(definition 1)

down[2] (doun), to or in a lower place. *adverb.*

draw (drô), **1** get; pull out: *To put on a good play, we must draw on the talents of everyone in the class.* **2** pull; drag; haul: *The horses draw the wagon.* **3** make a picture with pen, pencil, or chalk. **4** tie: *A game is a draw when neither side wins.* 1,2,3 *verb,* **drew, drawn, draw ing;** 4 *noun.*

drift (drift), **1** pile or be piled up by the wind: *The wind is so strong it's drifting the snow.* **2** snow or sand piled up by the wind. **3** carry or be carried along by air or water: *The breeze was drifting the rowboat toward shore.* **4** go along without knowing or caring where one is going. **5** meaning; direction of thought: *Please explain that again; I did not quite get the drift of your words.* 1,3,4 *verb,* 2,5 *noun.*

E e

e mer gen cy (i mėr/jən sē), **1** a sudden need for immediate action: *I keep a flashlight around for use in an emergency.* **2** for a time of sudden need: *When the brakes failed, the emergency brakes stopped the car.* 1 *noun, plural* **e mer gen cies;** 2 *adjective.*

en cour age (en kėr/ij), **1** give hope to: *The cheers of the crowd encouraged the team to try to win.* **2** give help to: *Sunlight encourages the growth of plants. verb.*

en vi ron ment (en vī/rən mənt), all the surrounding conditions that have to do with the growth of living things: *Plants will often grow differently in different environments. noun.*

e rupt (i rupt/), burst forth: *Lava and ashes erupted from the volcano.* See picture. *verb.*

volcano **erupting**

e vap o rate (i vap/ə rāt/), **1** turn into steam: *Boiling water evaporates fast.* **2** remove water from: *Heat is used to evaporate milk.* **3** vanish; disappear. *verb,* **e vap o rat ed, e vap o rat ing.**

ex pres sion (ek spresh/ən), **1** look that shows feeling: *The winners all had happy expressions on their faces.* **2** putting into words: *The expression of an idea. noun.*

F f

a hat	i it	oi oil	ch child	a in about
ā age	ī ice	ou out	ng long	e in taken
ä far	o hot	u cup	sh she	ə = { i in pencil
e let	ō open	u̇ put	th thin	o in lemon
ē equal	ô order	ü rule	ŦH then	u in circus
ėr term			zh measure	

fern (fėrn), kind of plant that has roots, stems, and leaves, but no flowers. The tiny seeds (called spores) grow in the little brown dots on the backs of the leaves. See picture. *noun.*

Boston **fern**

flock (flok), **1** group of animals of one kind keeping or feeding together: *a flock of sheep, a flock of geese, a flock of birds.* **2** a large number; crowd: *Visitors came to the zoo in flocks to see the new panda.* **3** go in a flock; keep in groups: *Sheep usually flock together.* **4** come crowding; crowd: *The children flocked around the ice-cream truck.* **1,2** *noun,* **3,4** *verb.*

for ma tion (fôr mā′shən), **1** way in which something is arranged; order: *The band marched in perfect formation.* **2** the forming, making, or shaping (of something). **3** thing formed: *Clouds are formations of tiny drops of water in the sky. noun.*

for mu la (fôr′myə lə), recipe: *a baby's formula. noun.*

frame (frām), **1** support over or around which something is built: *A house is built around a frame.* **2** Something that can be put around a picture: *a picture frame. noun.*

fret (fret), be or cause to be worried: *Some people fret over their mistakes. verb,* **fret ted, fret ting.**

fuel (fyü′əl), **1** anything that can be burned to make a useful fire. Coal, wood, and oil are fuels. **2** anything that keeps up or increases a feeling: *Insults will only add fuel to an argument. noun.*

fume (fyüm), **1** let off one's anger by complaining: *She fumed about the slowness of the train.* **2** gas or smoke especially if harmful or strong: *The fumes from the automobile nearly choked me.* **3** give off gas or smoke: *The candle fumed and then went out.* **1,3** *verb,* **fumed, fum ing;** **2** *noun.*

fuss (fus), **1** worry; worry when it is not necessary: *He fussed about his work in a nervous way.* **2** much bother about small matters; useless talk and worry. **1** *verb,* **2** *noun, plural* **fus ses.**

G g

gan der (gan′dər), a male goose. *noun.*

ge ol o gist (jē ol′ə jist), scientist who deals with the earth's crust, the outer part of the earth. *noun.*

gos ling (goz′ling), a young goose. See picture. *noun.*

gosling

grace ful (grās′fəl), **1** beautiful in form or movement: *a graceful dancer.* **2** pleasing; agreeable: *a graceful speech of thanks. adjective.*

graph (graf), line or picture showing how one thing depends on or changes with another. *You could draw a graph to show how your weight changes with each year. noun.*

greed y (grē′dē), wanting to get more than one's share; wanting to get a great deal. *adjective,* **greed i er, greed i est.**

H h

har bor (här′bər), **1** place where ships stay when they are not at sea. **2** any protected place. **3** have and keep in mind: *It's never good to harbor a grudge.* **1,2** *noun,* **3** *verb.*

harp (härp), a large stringed musical instrument played with the fingers. *noun.*

hel i cop ter (hel′ə kop′tər), aircraft without wings that is lifted from the ground and kept in the air by a blade that spins around on the top of the craft. See picture. *noun.*

helicopter

herd (hėrd), **1** a group of animals of one kind, especially large animals, keeping, feeding, or moving together: *a herd of cows, a herd of elephants.* **2** a large number of people. **3** join together: *Several people herded into the doorway.* **4** tend or take care of (cattle or sheep). **1,2** *noun,* **3,4** *verb.*

hide¹ (hīd), an animal's skin. *noun.*

hide² (hīd), put out of sight; keep out of sight. *verb,* **hid, hid den** *or* **hid, hid ing.**

hint (hint), **1** a slight sign or clue: *A small cloud gave a hint of a coming storm.* **2** show, but not directly: *She hinted that she was tired by yawning several times.* **1** *noun,* **2** *verb.*

hip po pot a mus (hip′ə pot′ə məs), a large, thick-skinned, almost hairless animal found in and near the rivers of Africa. It often weighs as much as four tons. See picture. *noun, plural* **hip po pot a mus es** *or* **hip po pot a mi** (hip′ə pot′ə mī). (*Hippopotamus* is from a Greek word meaning "river horse.")

hippopotamus

hiss (his), **1** make a sound like *ss,* or like a drop of water on a hot stove: *The cat hissed at the dog.* **2** a sound like *ss: Hisses were heard from the angry crowd.* **1** *verb,* **2** *noun, plural* **hiss es.**

hol low (hol′ō), **1** having nothing or only air inside: *A tube or pipe is hollow.* **2** shaped like a bowl or cup: *a hollow dish for soup.* **3** a hollow place; hole: *a hollow in the road.* **4** bend or dig out a hollow shape: *She hollowed a whistle out of wood.* **1,2** *adjective,* **3** *noun,* **4** *verb.*

hom i ny (hom′ə nē), a Native American name for a food that is made by boiling a type of dried corn, called squaw corn, in water. *noun.*

hub cap (həb′kap′), a round metal cover. It fits over the bolts that hold a car wheel to a car. See picture. *noun.*

hubcap

hu mane (hyü mān′), kind; not cruel: *I believe in the humane treatment of animals. adjective.*

a hat	i it	oi oil	ch child	⎧ a in about
ā age	ī ice	ou out	ng long	⎪ e in taken
ä far	o hot	u cup	sh she	ə = ⎨ i in pencil
e let	ō open	u̇ put	th thin	⎪ o in lemon
ē equal	ô order	ü rule	ᴛʜ then	⎩ u in circus
ėr term			zh measure	

J j

jam (jam), **1** many people or things crowded together so that they cannot move freely: *He was late because he got caught in a traffic jam.* **2** press or squeeze tightly between two things: *The ship was jammed between two rocks.* **3** press or squeeze (things or people) tightly together. **1** *noun,* **2,3** *verb,* **jammed, jam ming.**

I i

Ice land (īs′land), a large island in the North Atlantic Ocean between Greenland and Denmark. *noun.*

i dly (ī′dlē), doing nothing: *He spent the day idly on the beach. adverb.*

il lus tra tion (il′ə strā′shən), **1** picture, diagram, or map used to explain something. **2** story or example used to make clear or explain something: *The illustration showed how the ship was built. noun.*

in cred i ble (in kred′ə bəl), beyond belief: *The racing car rounded the curve with incredible speed. adjective.*

in gre di ent (in grē′dē ənt), one of the parts of a mixture: *The ingredients of a cake usually include eggs, sugar, and flour. noun.*

in spire (in spīr′), fill with a thought or feeling: *A chance to try again inspired us with hope. verb,* **in spired, in spir ing.**

in ter twine (in′tər twīn′), twist one (thing) around another: *The branches of the two trees intertwined. verb,* **in ter twined, in ter twin ing.**

L l

las so (las′ō), **1** a long rope with a noose at the end, used for catching horses and cattle. **2** catch with a lasso. See picture. **1** *noun, plural* **las sos** *or* **las soes;** **2** *verb.*

lasso (definition 1)

la va (lä′və), **1** hot, melted rock that flows from a volcano. **2** rock formed by the cooling of this melted rock. Some lavas are hard and glassy; others are light and porous. *noun.*

lev er (lev′ər *or* lē′vər), a stick or bar used to raise heavy objects on one end of the bar by pushing down at the other end. *noun.*

limp[1] (limp), not stiff; ready to bend or droop: *Spaghetti gets limp when you cook it. adjective.*

limp[2] (limp), **1** the walk of a leg or foot that is hurt. **2** walk with a limp: *After my fall, I limped for days.* **1** *noun,* **2** *verb.*

loom (lüm), appear dimly; appear as large or dangerous: *A large iceberg loomed through the thick, gray fog. verb.*

loon (lün), a large diving bird with webbed feet. It eats fish. Loons have a loud, wild cry. See picture. *noun.*

loon

luke warm (lük′wôrm′), **1** neither hot nor cold. **2** showing little excitement: *a lukewarm greeting. adjective.*

M m

ma hog a ny (mə hog′ə nē), **1** wood from a mahogany tree. **2** tree that grows in warm areas of America. Its wood is reddish brown: *Because mahogany looks beautiful when it is polished, it is often used to make furniture.* **3** dark reddish brown. **1,2** *noun, plural* **ma hog a nies; 3** *adjective.*

mane (mān), the long, heavy hair on the back or around the neck of a horse or lion. *noun.*

man tel (man′tl), shelf above a fireplace. *noun.*

marsh (märsh), low land covered at times by water; swamp. *noun, plural* **marsh es.**

mi cro phone (mī′krə fōn), something that makes sounds louder: *The speaker spoke into the microphone so that the people in the back could hear her. noun.*

mi gra tion (mī grā′shən) **1** going from one area to another with the change in seasons: *When birds move to warmer places in the winter, it is called migration. noun.*

Min ne so ta (min′ə sō′tə), one of the midwestern states of the United States. *noun.* (*Minnesota* was named for the Minnesota River. This word came from Native American words meaning "sky-colored water.")

moc ca sin (mok′ə sən), **1** a soft leather shoe without a heel. **2** a snake found in the southern part of the United States. See picture. *noun.*

moccasin snake (definition 2)

mol ten (mōlt′n), melted by heat. *adjective.*

mon strous (mon′strəs), **1** huge; very large. **2** shocking; horrible; dreadful. *adjective.*

moose (müs), animal somewhat like a large deer, living in Canada and the northern part of the United States. The male has a large head. *noun, plural* **moose.** (*Moose* comes from a Native American word meaning "he strips off the bark." The moose was called this because it strips off and eats the bark of trees.)

N n

nat ur al (nach′ər əl), **1** having such great talent or skill in something that it seems as if one was born with that skill. **2** produced by nature: *a natural resource. adjective.*

night in gale (nīt′n gāl), a small reddish-brown bird of Europe. The nightingale sings sweetly at night as well as in the daytime. *noun.*

no ble (nō′bəl), **1** excellent; fine; magnificent: *Niagara Falls is a noble sight.* **2** high and great by birth, rank, or title: *a noble family.* **3** person high and great by birth, rank, or title. **1,2** *adjective,* **no bler, no blest; 3** *noun.*

noose (nüs), **1** loop with a slip knot that tightens as the string or rope is pulled. See picture. *noun.*

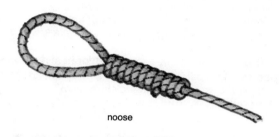

noose

north ern lights (nôr ŦHərn līts), bands of light appearing in the sky in northern areas.

O o

oak (ōk), **1** a kind of tree or shrub found in most parts of the world, having nuts that are called acorns. **2** its hard, strong wood, used in building and flooring. **3** of an oak: *oak leaves.* **4** made of oak wood: *an oak table.* **1,2** *noun,* **3,4** *adjective.*

oat (ōt), a kind of cereal grass whose grain is used in making oatmeal and as a food for horses and other farm animals. *noun.*

oc cu py (ok′yə pī), **1** take up; fill: *The building occupies an entire block. The lessons occupy the morning.* **2** keep busy. **3** take possession of: *The enemy occupied our fort.* **4** hold; have in use: *A judge occupies an important position.* **5** live in: *They occupy that house.* verb, **oc cu pied, oc cu py ing.**

o pin ion (ə pin′yən) **1** a person's own thoughts or feelings about whether something or someone is good or bad: *I have a good opinion of her.* **2** what one thinks: *I try to learn the facts and form my own opinions. noun.*

or bit (ôr′bit), **1** travel around the earth or some other planet, star, or moon in a set path: *An astronaut orbits the earth in a spaceship.* **2** path of the earth or any one of the planets around the sun. **3** path of any planet, moon, or star around another planet, moon, or star. **1** *verb,* **2,3** *noun.*

out rage (out′rāj), **1** offend greatly; insult: *The girl was outraged by her friend's selfish behavior.* **2** an act that shows no care for the feelings of others. **1** *verb,* **out raged, out raging; 2** *noun.*

P p

pale (pāl), **1** not bright; dim: *pale blue.* **2** without much color; whitish. **3** turn pale. **1,2** *adjective,* **pal er, pal est; 3** *verb,* **paled, pal ing.**

pat ter (pat′ər), **1** make quick taps: *Bare feet pattered along the hard floor.* **2** series of quick taps or the sound they make: *the patter of raindrops.* **1** *verb,* **2** *noun.*

ped es tal (ped′i stəl), **1** block of wood, stone, or metal on which a statue or other things stand. See picture. **2** base of a tall lamp. *noun.*

pedestal (definition 1)

per son al (pėr′sə nəl), **1** about a person; private matters: *My feelings are personal to me.* **2** belonging to a person: *a personal letter.* **3** done in person; directly by oneself, not through others or by letter: *a personal visit. adjective.*

pes ter (pes′tər), **1** annoy; trouble. **2** act like a pest; bother: *Don't pester me with foolish questions. verb.*

pit y (pit′ē), **1** thing to be sorry for: *It is a pity to stay indoors when the weather is fine.* **2** the feeling of being sorry for another. **3** feel sorry for another. **1,2** *noun,* **3** *verb,* **pit ied, pit y ing.**

plaque (plak), thin, flat plate of metal or wood that is hung on walls. Very often it is presented as an award, and a description of the award and the name of the person receiving it are written on it. *noun.*

plume (plüm), **1** a large, long feather. **2** smooth or arrange the feathers of: *The eagle plumed its wing.* **1** *noun,* **2** *verb,* **plumed, plum ing.**

pol i cy (pol′ə sē), plan of action; way of doing things: *It is a poor policy to promise more than you can do. noun, plural* **pol i cies.**

pol lu tion (pə lü′shən) a making dirty or not pure: *Garbage is a form of pollution. noun.*

pow er ful (pou′ər fəl), having great strength or force; strong: *The United States is a very powerful nation. adjective.*

pow wow (pou′wou′), **1** meeting of Native Americans at which there is dancing, eating, and celebrating. **2** hold a powwow; talk in a meeting, **1** *noun,* **2** *verb.*

prair ie (prer′ē), a large area of flat or rolling land with grass but few or no trees. See picture. *noun.*

prairie

proc ess (pros′es), **1** set of actions or changes in a special order: *By what process is cloth made from wool?* **2** treat or prepare by some special set of actions: *This cloth has been processed to make it waterproof.* **1** *noun, plural* **pro cess es;** **2** *verb.*

pro fes sion al (prə fesh′ə nəl), **1** making a business or job of something that others do for fun: *professional musicians.* **2** person who does this. **1** *adjective;* **2** *noun.*

prog ress (prog′res *for 1 and 3;* prə gres′ *for 2 and 4),* **1** growth; improvement: *the progress of science. The class showed progress in its studies.* **2** get better: *We progress in learning step by step.* **3** moving forward; going ahead: *make quick progress on a trip.* **4** move forward; go ahead: *The building of the new school progressed quickly.* **1,3** *noun,* **2,4** *verb.*

pro pane (prō′pān), a gas used for heating. *noun.*

pro pel (prə pel′), drive forward; force ahead: *propel a boat by oars.* See picture. *verb,* **pro pelled, pro pel ling.**

propelling a boat by oars

pro per ly (prop′ər lē), in a correct or fitting way: *If you want to eat properly, you must learn how to hold a fork and knife. adverb.*

pro test (prə test′ *for 1;* prō′test *for 2),* **1** be against something: *We protested against staying after school.* **2** statement against something. **1** *verb,* **2** *noun.*

R r

re ar range (rē′ə ranj′), **1** put in order again: *I had to rearrange my papers after the wind blew them on the floor.* **2** put in a new order or a new way: *They rearranged the furniture. verb,* **re ar ranged, re ar rang ing.**

re cess (rē′ses *or* ri ses′ for 1, ri ses′ for 2),
1 time during which work stops: *Our school has an
hour's recess at noon.* **2** take a recess: *The meeting
recessed for lunch.* **1** *noun,* **2** *verb.*

re ci pe (res′ə pē), set of directions for preparing
something to eat. *noun.*

re e lec tion or **re-e lec tion** (rē′i lek′shən),
choosing by a vote for the second time: *The
president worked hard toward his reelection. noun.*

re la tion (ri lā′shən), person who belongs to the
same family as another; relative. *noun.*

re lay race (rē′lā rās′), race in which a few
people compete as a team. Each person runs
or swims a part of the race. See picture. *noun.*

relay race

res er va tion (rez′ər va′shən), **1** land set aside
for a special reason. Some Native Americans live
on reservations. **2** arrangement to keep a thing for
a person: *Please make reservations for rooms at the
hotel. noun.*

re trieve (ri trēv′), **1** get again: *retrieve a lost
pocketbook.* **2** find and bring to a person: *Some
dogs can be trained to retrieve things.* verb,
re trieved, re triev ing.

rhi noc er os (rī nos′ər əs), a large, thick-skinned
animal with hoofs and one or two upright horns on
the snout. *noun, plural* **rhi noc er os es** *or*
rhi noc er os. (*Rhinoceros* is from Greek words
meaning "nose" and "horn.")

a hat	i it	oi oil	ch child	⎧ a in about
ā age	ī ice	ou out	ng long	⎪ e in taken
ä far	o hot	u cup	sh she	ə = ⎨ i in pencil
e let	ō open	u̇ put	th thin	⎪ o in lemon
ē equal	ô order	ü rule	ᴛʜ then	⎩ u in circus
ėr term			zh measure	

rock et (rok′it), **1** go very, very fast: *The racing
car rocketed across the finish line.* **2** a tube that is a
form of fireworks and shoots into the air. Larger
rockets can send spaceships to outer space. See
picture. **1** *verb,* **2** *noun.*

space **rocket**
(definition 2)

root (rüt), **1** part of a plant that grows down into
the soil and holds water. **2** part from which things
grow: *Hair grows out of roots in the skin.* **3** word
from which other words are made. *Room* is the
root of *roominess. noun.*

roots (definition 1)

347

rum ble (rum′bəl), **1** make a deep, heavy, lasting sound: *The thunder rumbled all night long.* **2** a heavy, lasting sound. **3** move with such a sound: *The train rumbled along over the tracks.* **1,3** *verb,* **rum bled, rum bling; 2** *noun.*

S s

safe (sāf), **1** place, usually a strong, locked metal box, for keeping things protected. **2** free from harm or danger. **1** *noun,* **2** *adjective.*

sanc tu ar y (sangk′chü er′ē), a place that is safe and protected: *The government sets aside sanctuaries for birds and animals.* See picture. *noun.*

sanctuary

scoop (sküp), **1** take up or out with a scoop, or as a scoop does: *You scoop up snow with your hands to make snowballs.* **2** tool like a small shovel for dipping out or shoveling up things. **3** amount taken up at one time by a scoop. **1** *verb,* **2,3** *noun.*

screech (skrēch), **1** a shrill, sharp scream or sound: *The car made a screech as it turned the corner.* **2** cry out sharply in a high voice. **1** *noun,* *plural* **screech es; 2** *verb.*

scuf fle (skuf′əl), **1** go or move in a hurried and mixed-up way. **2** a movement that is hurried and mixed up: *a scuffle of feet.* **1** *verb,* **2** *noun.*

sec re tar y (sek′rə ter′ē), **1** person who writes letters and keeps things in order for a person, company, club, and the like: *The secretary typed a letter for the manager.* **2** person in charge of part of the government. The Secretary of State is in charge of dealing with countries. *noun, plural* **sec re tar ies.**

shawl (shôl), a square or oblong piece of cloth to be worn about the shoulders or head. See picture. *noun.*

shawl

shoot (shüt), **1** a new part growing out; young branch: *See the new shoots on that bush.* **2** fire or use (a gun, arrow, and the like): *shoot a bow and arrow.* **3** take (a picture) with a camera. **1** *noun,* **2,3** *verb,* **shot, shoot ing.**

shrill (shril), **1** high and sharp in sound: *Some screams are shrill noises.* **2** make a shrill sound. **1** *adjective,* **2** *verb.*

side wind (sīd′wīnd), move part of the body to the side with great force, making a whiplike motion with the other part of the body. *verb.*

skel e ton (skel′ə tən), **1** bones of a body, fitted together in their natural places. **2** frame: *the steel skeleton of a building. noun.* (Skeleton comes from Greek words meaning "a dried-up body.")

skill (skil), **1** ability gained by practice or knowledge: *It takes skill to tune a piano. noun.*

slen der (slen′dər), **1** long and thin; not big around; slim: *a slender child.* **2** slight; small: *a slender hope. adjective.*

slump (slump), stand in a drooping manner; slouch. *verb*

snarl[1] (snärl), **1** growl sharply and show one's teeth: *The dog snarled at the cat.* **2** a sharp, angry growl. **1** *verb,* **2** *noun.*

snarl[2] (snärl), **1** tangle: *snarls in your hair.* **2** tangle; jam. *noun.*

soil¹ (soil), ground; earth; dirt: *Roses grow best in rich soil.* See picture. *noun.*

soil (definition 1)

soil² (soil), make or become dirty. *verb.*

source (sôrs), person or place from which anything comes or is gotten: *Mines are the chief source of gold. noun.*

sou ve nir (sü′və nir′), something given or kept to remember someone or something that happened: *She bought a pair of moccasins as a souvenir of her trip out West. noun.*

spin dly (spin′dlē), growing into a long, slender branch or stem, often very weak. *adjective.*

spy (spī), **1** person who tries to get information about another person or group. **2** keep secret watch: *He saw two men spying on him from behind a tree.* **3** catch sight of; see: *She was the first to spy the mountains.* **1** *noun, plural* **spies;** **2,3** *verb,* **spied, spy ing.**

stam mer (stam′r), repeat the same sound when trying to speak. *verb.*

steer (stir), guide the way of: *steer a car. verb.*

stout ness (stout′nəs), the state of being fat and large. *noun.*

strive (strīv), try hard; work hard: *Strive to be very good at what you do. verb.*

stroke¹ (strōk), **1** single complete movement to be made again and again: *She swims with a strong stroke.* **2** act of striking: *I drove the nail in with several strokes of the hammer. noun.*

stroke² (strōk), move the hand gently along: *She likes to stroke her kitten. verb.*

sus pense (sə spens′), state of being uncertain: *The detective story kept me in suspense until the very end. noun.*

sus tain (sə stān′), **1** keep up; keep going: *She sustained her running speed for a long time.* **2** hold up: *Strong planks of wood sustain the roof and walls of a mine. verb.*

a hat	**i** it	**oi** oil	**ch** child	a in about
ā age	**ī** ice	**ou** out	**ng** long	e in taken
ä far	**o** hot.	**u** cup	**sh** she	ə = { i in pencil
e let	**ō** open	**u̇** put	**th** thin	o in lemon
ē equal	**ô** order	**ü** rule	**ᴛʜ** then	u in circus
ėr term			**zh** measure	

T t

tend¹ (tend), take care of; look after: *He tends shop for his parents. The cowboy tends the herd of cattle. verb.*

tend² (tend), **1** be likely: *Fruit tends to rot after a few days. I tend to sleep late on weekends.* **2** move (toward): *The road tends to the south here. verb.*

ten der (ten′dər), **1** delicate; not strong: *The leaves in spring are green and tender.* **2** not hard or tough; soft: *The meat is tender.* **3** kind; loving; gentle: *He spoke tender words to the baby. adjective.*

the a ter or **the a tre** (the′ə tər), place where plays are acted or movies are shown. *noun.*

thumb (thum), **1** turn pages quickly with a thumb or as if with a thumb: *I didn't read the book, I just thumbed through it.* **2** the short, thick finger of the hand. See picture. **1** *verb,* **thumbed, thumb ing;** **2** *noun.*

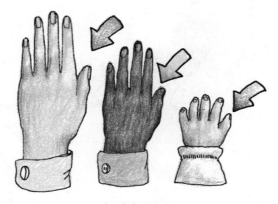

thumb (definition 2)

tilt (tilt), tip or cause to tip; slant: *You tilt your head when you bow. verb.*

tor na do (tôr nā′dō), a very strong and dangerous wind that twists around in a circle very fast. See picture. *noun, plural* **tor na does** or **tor na dos.**

tornado

tour na ment (tėr′nə mənt), contest of many persons in some sport: *a golf tournament. noun.*

tra di tion al (trə dish′ə nəl), of beliefs, stories, music, dance, and the like, handed down from parents to children and among groups, especially by word of mouth. *adjective.*

trom bone (trom′bōn), a brass wind instrument with a long sliding piece that helps change its sound. See picture. *noun.*

trombone

troupe (trüp), group or company, especially of actors, singers, or other performers. *noun.*

U u

ul ti mate (ul′tə mit), **1** last; final: *His ultimate answer was no.* **2** basic: *The brain is the ultimate source of ideas. adjective.*

un furl (un fėrl′), spread out; shake out; unfold: *Unfurl the flag. verb.*

ur ban (ėr′bən), **1** of or having something to do with cities and towns: *an urban area.* **2** living in a city or cities: *Many urban people take public transportation to work. adjective.*

V v

vine (vīn), a plant with a long, slender stem that grows along the ground or that climbs by attaching itself to a wall, tree, or other support. See picture. *noun.*

vines

vi ta min (vī′tə mən), any of certain special substances necessary for the normal growth of the body. Vitamins are found in all natural foods. *noun.*

vol ca no (vol kā′nō), an opening in the earth's crust through which steam, ashes, and lava are forced out. See picture. *noun, plural* **vol can noes** *or* **vol ca nos.**

a hat	**i** it	**oi** oil	**ch** child		a in about
ā age	**ī** ice	**ou** out	**ng** long		e in taken
ä far	**o** hot	**u** cup	**sh** she	**ə** =	i in pencil
e let	**ō** open	**u̇** put	**th** thin		o in lemon
ē equal	**ô** order	**ü** rule	**ŦH** then		u in circus
ėr term			**zh** measure		

W w

wad dle (wod′l), walk with short steps and a swaying motion, like a duck. *verb,* **wad dled, wad dling.**

weave (wēv), **1** form (threads or strips) into a thing or fabric. People weave thread into cloth, straw into hats, and reeds into baskets. See picture. **2** make out of thread, strips, or strands of the same material. *verb.*

wedge (wej), pack in tightly; squeeze: *His foot was wedged between the rocks. verb.*

wheeze (hwēz), **1** breathe with difficulty and a whistling sound: *Running made him so out of breath he began to wheeze.* **2** a whistling sound caused by difficult breathing. **1** *verb,* **2** *noun.*

whim per (hwim′pər), **1** a soft, sad cry with low, broken sounds. **2** to cry in this way. **1** *noun,* **2** *verb.*

wig wam (wig′wom), hut made with poles covered by bark, mats, or skins. See picture. *noun.*

wigwams

weaving a rainbow of colors (definition 1)

Y y

yank (yangk), **1** pull with a sudden motion; jerk; tug: *I yanked the door open.* **2** sudden pull; jerk; tug. **1** *verb,* **2** *noun.*

(Acknowledgments continued from page 2)

"The Bravest Babysitter" adapted from THE BRAVEST BABYSITTER by Barbara Greenberg. Copyright © 1977 by Barbara Greenberg. Reprinted by permission of The Dial Press.

From "The Case of the Broken Globe" and "The Case of the Secret Pitch." Reprinted by permission of the publisher Elsevier/Nelson Books. From the book ENCYCLOPEDIA BROWN TAKES THE CASE by Donald J. Sobol. Copyright © 1973 by Donald J. Sobol.

"When I Grow Up" from "When I Grow Up" from JONATHAN BLAKE by William Wise. Reprinted by permission of Curtis Brown, Ltd.

"Kitchen Window Gardens" is an adaptation of pages 80–82 of GROWING A GARDEN INDOORS AND OUT (text only) by Katherine N. Cutler. Copyright © 1973 by Katherine N. Cutler. By permission of Lothrop, Lee & Shepard Co. (A Division of William Morrow & Co.)

"Kevin Cloud, Chippewa Boy in the City" from KEVIN CLOUD, CHIPPEWA BOY IN THE CITY by Carol Ann Bales. © 1972 by Carol Ann Bales. Used with the permission of Contemporary Books, Inc., Chicago.

"How Old Is Old?" from HOW OLD IS OLD by Leonore Klein. Copyright 1967 by Harvey House, Inc. Reprinted by permission of the author.

Adapted by permission of Four Winds Press, a division of Scholastic Magazines, Inc., from FRECKLE JUICE by Judy Blume. Copyright © 1971 by Judy Blume.

Glossary entries and skill lesson dictionary entries taken or adapted from SCOTT, FORESMAN BEGINNING DICTIONARY. Copyright © 1979, Scott, Foresman and Company, Glenview, Illinois. All Rights Reserved.

ILLUSTRATIONS

Cover: Joel Naprstek
Pages 8–20, Bernard Waber; 21, James Dyekman; 22–24, Jerry Zimmerman; 25–32, Michael W. Adams; 33–44, Pat Stewart; 45–47, Jerry Zimmerman; 48–60, John O'Brien; 61–71, Margot Apple; 72, James Dyekman; 82–84, Jerry Zimmerman; 85–92, Anthony Rao; 93–101, Kathy Allert; 102–111, Pat Stewart; 112, James Dyekman; 113–116, Jerry Zimmerman; 117–128, Lane Yerkes; 141–144, Jerry Zimmerman; 145–154, Anthony Rao; 156, 162, 166, 167, Ernest H. Shepard; 170–180, Ann Blades; 181, James Dyekman; 182–189, Kinuko Craft; 190–193, Jerry Zimmerman; 194–204, Lisa Bonforte; 205–215, Will Harmuth; 216–228, Diane Redfield Massie; 229, James Dyekman; 230–244, Jerry Zimmerman; 245–255, Will Harmuth; 256–258, Jerry Zimmerman; 259–270, Anthony Rao; 271–279, James Dyekman; 280–288, Maggie MacGowan; 289–291, Jerry Zimmerman; 292–304, Carol Ann Bales; 305–316, Christopher Santoro; 317–334, Margot Apple; 336, 338 (left), Riegler/Fredric Lewis; 339, James Dyekman; 341, 343 (right), 344, 345 (left), Kathy Allert; 346 (left), James Dyekman; 347 (left), Kathy Allert; 347 (bottom right), James Dyekman; 348 (right), 349 (right), Kathy Allert; 350 (bottom left), James Dyekman; 351, Kathy Allert.

PHOTOGRAPHS

Pages 76, 78, Rosemarie Hausherr; 129, Jack Vartoogian; 130, Martha Swope; 131–138, Marbeth; 139, Jack Vartoogian; 337 (left), Lambert/Fredric Lewis; 337 (right), Muir/Fredric Lewis; 338 (right), Riegler/Fredric Lewis; 340 (left), Lambert/Fredric Lewis; 340 (right), Fredric Lewis; 342 (left), Azzara/Fredric Lewis; 342 (right), Toker/Fredric Lewis; 343 (left) Riegler/Fredric Lewis; 345 (right), Meston/Fredric Lewis; 346 (right), Sworger/Fredric Lewis; 347 (top right), 348 (left), Meston/Fredric Lewis; 349 (left), Carlin/Fredric Lewis; 350 (top left), Lambert/Fredric Lewis; 350 (right), Dean/Fredric Lewis.

STUDIO

Kaeser and Wilson Design, Ltd.

X